W9-CEM-847

Pendulums

Pendulums

How to use them for
dowsing and divination

Emily Anderson

ARCTURUS

For Alice, for the many interesting
esoteric conversations over the years,
and Mel, for all your love and friendship.

All images courtesy of Shutterstock.

ARCTURUS

This edition published in 2020 by Arcturus Publishing Limited
26/27 Bickels Yard, 151–153 Bermondsey Street,
London SE1 3HA

ISBN: 978-1-83857-290-7
AD008214UK

Printed in China

Contents

Introduction

Mention *dowsing* to anyone and the first thing they'll think of is someone holding sticks or rods as they twist and jerk towards water. *Pendulum dowsing* conjures up an image of a ring on string being dangled over a pregnant woman's bump to discover the gender of the child. Both of these visions are accurate depictions, but a mere fraction of what this book is all about – dowsing, especially with a pendulum, is about so much more.

Dowsing is the art of finding that which is hidden – whether that's water, the answers to certain questions or your door keys. It was traditionally done by holding sticks, but then using a pendulum was found to give even more accurate results. A pendulum is, most simply, a symmetrical weight on the end of a piece of string, held between thumb and forefinger. Pendulums naturally move freely in different ways to indicate a positive and negative response.

This guide to pendulum dowsing will help you choose your first pendulum, get comfortable with it, and tune into its possible responses to various situations and enquiries. It will also give you many ways to prepare yourself before any dowsing session, calming the mind, centring yourself, and being open to all possible outcomes. Pendulum dowsing is as much about letting go of preconceived ideas and tapping into your intuition, as it is about receiving answers to all the questions you may have.

When tuned into your pendulum you can ask it questions about anything. It can help you with life choices, food decisions, guidance on the right path to take in your career, love life and spiritual purpose. You can use a pendulum to help reorganise your home, create the perfect garden, find lost objects and even locate missing pets.

Take your pendulum with you to sacred sites or ancient ruins and it will help you feel the magical energies that gather there. In time, you can even use it to search spooky places and uncover deeper mysteries, all the while developing your spiritual side and psychic abilities, if that is what you desire.

Dowsing has traditionally been used in many societies around the world in an attempt to locate water in dry regions. This began with the use of dowsing rods, as shown above, but you can get the same results with the use of a pendulum.

Of course, you don't want to rely solely on your pendulum to make decisions for you, whether large or small. You must still use your own instinct, wisdom and reason to work out what's best for you or anyone else you may be dowsing for.

Pendulums can be made of many different materials, with crystals being particularly popular.

You must *always* seek proper medical attention for anything that concerns you about your health or well-being. But you can ask your pendulum to help you with aspects of your health, including working out which supplements to take, easing pain, and balancing your chakras.

While pendulum dowsing is most definitely to be taken seriously – it is not a party trick in any way – it is also something to be enjoyed. Used carefully and wisely, it can lead you confidently through life, enabling you to discover and follow your dreams, and help you and others make the right decisions in so many wonderful ways.

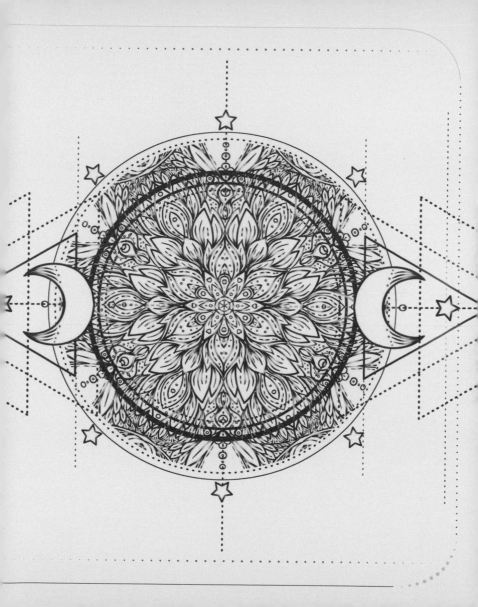

Part One

PENDULUMS
IN
THEORY

The history of pendulums

ANCIENT BEGINNINGS

The use of pendulums and dowsing, especially with rods or twigs, goes back many centuries to our early ancestors. In cave paintings in the Northern African mountains of Algeria there is evidence of dowsers, most likely searching for underground sources of water, to ensure people settled near their most precious resource for drinking, cooking and washing. The earliest such images of people dowsing with a forked stick in their hands are dated at around 6000BCE.

Other sources suggest a famous diviner lived in Ancient China, as depicted on a statue of the Chinese Emperor Kwang Su from about 2200BCE. Ancient Egyptian papyri and paintings also show dowsers searching for precious metals and gemstones, essential to the expansion of their culture.

Early Roman discoveries from Europe in the 1st century CE suggest pendulums were used at this time. The first recorded evidence of pendulums being used for divining decisions as well as for minerals and water, comes from the Roman 1st century CE writer Marcellinus. He describes a ring on a thread hanging from a tripod, around the circumference of which was a circle of letters of the Roman alphabet for the ring to swing towards to spell out the answers to the questions asked.

Cave paintings in the Algerian section of the Sahara Desert have been found that are said to show humans dowsing with sticks.

It is said that Cleopatra had dowsers with her at all times and used their services to locate gold.

This method of finding out answers using a pendulum carried on until the Middle Ages, and woodcuts from this time depict diviners or 'oscillators', as they were then known. However, in 1326 Pope John XII forbade the practice of 'the use of a ring to obtain answers in the manner of the Devil', and it was then considered 'nonsense' at best, or worse connected to witchcraft and punishable by death.

Despite this declaration, the first image of a dowser in literature was published, in 1540, in a book on mining and metallurgy called *De Re Metallica* by Georgius Agricola. It shows a man with a forked stick searching for mineral deposits in the earth. However, by 1584, Reginald Scot in *The Discoverie of Witchcraft* states that dowsing rods, 'be mere toys to mock apes, and have no commendable device [purpose].'

This image, which appeared in a book called De Re Metallica *in 1540, is the first depiction of a dowser to be found in literature.*

SCIENCE AND ART

How wrong could he be? Around this same time, Italian scientist Galileo Galilei was inspired by the swinging chandelier in Pisa Cathedral to study the motion of the pendulum and its ability to keep time. He used pendulums made from different materials as his gravity measuring instruments. This led him to conceive and design the first pendulum clock, although he didn't see it built before he died. It was Dutch mathematician and physicist Christiaan Huygens who built the first clock with a swinging pendulum to mark the accurate passing of time in 1656.

Galileo's experiments with a pendulum eventually led to scientists being able to calculate the shape of the Earth and, in the case of French

physicist Foucault in 1851, prove that the Earth spins and takes 24 hours to do so. It is also believed that other great artists and thinkers including Leonardo da Vinci and Albert Einstein used pendulum dowsing in their work. It was certainly a fascination for many great minds.

At the same time as pendulums were being used to explore science, people were still very interested in alchemy, magic and dowsing as a natural art. Several academic works, often by French priests, were published in this, and subsequent, centuries. This began a long history of the French, in particular, experimenting with and researching dowsing. In the 1750s, scientists here

Galileo used pendulums to help him calculate the shape of the Earth.

looked into the possible connection between dowsing and electricity. Over 100 years later, the use of the divining wand was still popular and interesting enough for the Academy of Sciences in Paris to set up a commission to examine its powers.

Images of dowsers with their forked sticks can be seen in French publications through the ages, as well as on old coins and statues, showing the constant interest in, and importance of, dowsers. In the German Bergbau museum, for example, there is a Meissen porcelain figure of a dowser wearing a miner's uniform, that dates from the 18th century.

In the 19th century, it was written about in the *Quarterly Review*, when geologist Dr Hutton observed the facial contortions and power of the force moving the rods, when Lady Milbanke, mother-in-law to Lord Byron, dowsed for water in an experiment in London. Hutton saw that 'a **degree of agitation was visible in her face when she first made the experiment; she says this agitation was great,' whenever she practised her art.** But Byron himself didn't sound quite as impressed when he wrote of her death: 'She is at last gone to a place where she can no longer dowse.'

Naturally, dowsing went with the European settlers to America, Australia and South Africa to help them locate underground water sources and existing wells to base their towns around. So many Hollywood Westerns fairly accurately depict pioneers to new lands, dowsing, stick jerking, as they writhe with the force pulling the dowsing stick towards the water source.

DOWSING NEVER DIES

Until Victorian times, dowsing was regarded, and respected, as a natural art. But as the Industrial Revolution unfolded, people moved from the countryside to cities and towns where municipal water systems meant no one needed to dowse for water supplies. With the worship of science growing stronger, this ancient practice dwindled to become a rural novelty or something children did for fun before they grew too old to question it working.

Yet that wasn't quite the end of dowsing or pendulums. The early 1900s saw a revival in their use, especially in France. Another priest Abbé Bouly, who lived near the Channel, found water sources for French and other European manufacturers before using his skills to discover unexploded shells in the ground after the First World War. It is said that even when the bombs were in the ground, he could tell the difference between the German and Allied ones.

Abbé Bouly carried on exploring dowsing throughout his life, including experiments in hospitals where he used a pendulum to identify different microbe cultures in various test tubes as accurately as if he'd used a microscope. With another priest, Abbé Mermet, Bouly researched pendulum dowsing in health and medical fields. Bouly was awarded the French Legion of Honour in 1950, and Mermet is still considered the most famous pendulum expert. Learning to dowse from his grandfather, he ended up working on various famous cases including helping to find missing children and solving archaeological enigmas for the Vatican. His book *How I Proceed in the Discovery of Near or Distant Water, Metals, Hidden Objects and Illnesses* is seen as a classic guide to dowsing. He also worked with another priest, a missionary in Brazil, on medical diagnosis and treatment using the pendulum, a method still used by alternative health practitioners today.

Dowsing for water came back into use after World War II, as the cheapest and most accurate way of finding water sources during the rebuilding and expansion of bombed towns and cities. Water-diviner Colonel Kenneth Merrylees had used his dowsing skills in World War II to find unexploded bombs that had penetrated deep into the ground. It ignited interest in the benefits and capabilities of dowsing once again.

In 1959, American dowser Verne Cameron used a pendulum to successfully pinpoint every US Navy and Russian submarine – on a map. Again, using a map, he deciphered which submarines in the Pacific Ocean were

American, Russian or belonged to other countries. This marked him out as a security risk according to the CIA, who stopped him leaving the country when asked to go to South Africa to help them find minerals and other valuable resources.

In more recent years, the military have recognised dowsing skills to help locate enemy tunnels, submarines or mines at sea, and unexploded bombs on land. In the Vietnam war, the US marines were shown how to use pendulums to help them find tunnels and land mines. Sometimes secretly, but more often openly, governments, oil companies and even pharmaceutical companies employ dowsers. In Britain, there are more than 20 dowsing societies, and in the US over 70 chapters connected to the American Society of Dowsers, while in Russia you can even study for a masters degree in dowsing.

It would seem pendulums and dowsing are becoming more accepted nowadays, and in areas of life where previously they would have been rejected. But there has always been a section of society who have used them for more spiritual purposes, for making decisions, for choosing healing modalities and for choosing the best path to take. Pendulum dowsing is still a fascination to many and a relied upon method of making decisions. But how does it actually work?

How does pendulum dowsing work?

Despite centuries of exploration and experimentation, exactly how pendulum dowsing works is still a bit of a mystery. Although leading artists and scientists of their era, such as Leonardo da Vinci and Albert Einstein, used the pendulum in their work, even they didn't hit on exactly how dowsing works.

Galileo used pendulums made of different materials to research gravity, the force of attraction of the Earth. He found out that the swinging weight of any material usually goes towards the direction where the attraction of the Earth is greatest. But more recent science shows that it's not just this force that sets the ball moving or that the 'oscillations' are pure chance. Other factors play a part.

It has long been believed that the vibration transmitted from water, minerals and other resources causes the dowsing rod or pendulum to move, in the right hands. Mind you, the American Society of Dowsers says everyone can dowse. Out of 25 adults, between two and five people will instantly be able to do it, the rest will also be confident with practice. Is dowsing as innate a skill as our intuition, something we all have the ability to use, even if we doubt or suppress it? It was always seen as a natural skill that was simply practised more by some than by others, so that some people got better at it – the same as with painting, sculpting or any sports, for example. But it has long baffled our brains trying to figure out how it works.

From the mid 18th century and throughout the 19th century, scientists explored a connection between dowsing and electricity – another unseen but mighty powerful source of energy. Did underground water sources or unexploded bombs radiate an electrical frequency that made the pendulum move? Magnetic attractions and influences were also examined as plausible reasons for the pendulum oscillating towards that to which it is magnetically attracted.

Now, it is more likely believed to be electromagnetic frequency, or radiation, that is emitted from whatever the pendulum is trying to pick up, a similar energy to that which pulses from electrical gadgets and phones. But this still doesn't explain the pendulum's ability to find missing objects, locate things on a map, or answer questions about our health, relationships or purpose.

For these phenomenon there seems to be an intrinsic link between the pendulum and us. But is this our bodies pulsing a frequency that resonates with the missing thing or the right answer to the question we are asking? Is it a kind of telekinesis moving the muscles of the body, as the hand holds the pendulum, that in turn makes it swing? But how does our body know

It was important to be able to locate underground sources of water in order to know where to dig wells.

what is good for us before our minds? These questions remain tantalisingly unanswered, but some have posited some theories.

Through the reverence of science above all else, we've placed so much importance on our brains that we've forgotten our bodies have a natural instinct for what we need or the right direction to go in. After all, our senses pick up 'bad vibes' about a place as soon as we enter, and can tell a lot from a person's energy – good or bad – upon first meeting them.

We know that energy in various forms exists. Some energies are so powerful they can destroy, such as that from lasers. We accept that X-ray energy is dangerous and should be used sparingly. In Eastern medicine and philosophy, it is accepted that as well as being physical matter, humans are also made up of energy. This energy interacts with everything around it, picking up information in ways we still don't definitely know, beyond our five senses. Why couldn't that energy be expressed by the pendulum to guide us in the right direction?

So is this invisible energy altogether more mystical? After all, to 'divine' is to uncover that which is hidden, and pendulum divination does just that. It's definitely connected to an extra sensory perception or intuition. But what is that anyway? Is it simply an inner guidance from deep within our soul, or our heart's desire pulsing electromagnetic waves so strong it can't be ignored? What if we are connecting with a universal life force, the collective unconscious that knows everything ahead of time?

Or could we be tapping into the Akashic records? This is believed to be an etheric library, of sorts, where everything that has ever happened in all past lives, or is yet to come in the future, is stored and can be revealed to you. Many people access these etheric records through hypnosis or guided meditation, but could dowsing help tune us into this abundance of information?

To dowse or divine effectively, you have to still the mind and connect with your centre. From this still point of awareness it is possible to hear an inner voice or get a strong sense of knowing the right answer or way forward. Could that guidance be coming from a higher power, spirit guides or even angels? Traditionally, divination meant getting in touch with the *divus*, or gods within, to reveal and inspire the direction of your path. Who is to say we aren't guided by beings of light who communicate with us using dowsing as one of the countless techniques with which they impart their messages. Using a pendulum to find answers definitely brings to light information or perspectives previously unseen. It adds more to a soul-searching conundrum than purely rational thinking alone, often revealing issues that lie hidden in the deepest parts of our being.

Connecting with this deeper power though the pendulum can help you get to the root of blockages to certain paths, examine your deeper motives in life, and know yourself better than ever before. Alternative health practitioners, in particular, use dowsing to work out the root cause of ill health and tune into the body's innate sense of knowing what it needs for optimum well-being.

Once you start to use the pendulum regularly, you will tune into this energy to help guide you through life. And whether it's your body's cells radiating information, your heart pulsing electrical impulses of what it desires, or angels guiding you forward, it is energy, it is real and it works – so why not explore and use it more?

What materials should it be made from?

Dowsing sticks, the earliest tool for water or mineral divining, were made from a forked stick or twigs from trees. The protective rowan tree was used for finding metals, while hazel, traditionally associated with wisdom, was best for locating water. Held loosely in the hands at a right angle to the earth, a person would walk over land until the sticks moved in a certain way – often jerking or pointing directly to the source – above the water or minerals deep in the ground.

The pendulum, which came later, is preferred for dowsing for objects, using a map, and for answering questions. They are always made from a symmetrical, non-magnetic object, such as a ring, metal or wooden weight or a crystal, tied from a centre point to a lightweight chain or string. This thread can be made from any natural material, such as finely-spun silk or cotton, or a silver chain with circular links of equal size so the energy between your pendulum and

you transfers smoothly. Whatever it is made from, the length of this chain or string is the most important aspect. Too short and the weight might not move as freely as it needs to, but too long and your personal contact with the pendulum can be lost.

With the chain or thread held firmly but gently between thumb and index-finger, the weight at the end of the thread oscillates according to the direction of the object being sought, or spins one way for a "no" answer, another for 'yes', depending on how it has been calibrated. (More on this on page 44.)

In theory, you can divine with anything heavy enough not to get blown about in the wind if dowsing outside, such as a key, curtain ring or washer from a tap. In fact, the English archaeologist, parapsychologist and writer Thomas Lethbridge, a famous dowsing advocate, claimed he had successfully used a piece of chewing gum attached to a thread for dowsing!

But it's much nicer to have a pendulum made of a material you like, that can be imbued with significance and energy from you every time you use it. This could be some of the wood mentioned above carved into a diamond shape suspended from a piece of string. You might be keen on a more traditional, shiny, brass, upside-down tear-drop-shaped weight. Or you might prefer one made from your favourite crystal, which is even more receptive to being charged with your energy or with an intention for a specific purpose, such as dowsing for healing.

With a crystal pendulum, the properties of different gemstones will add to the information gleaned in a dowsing. Rose quartz pendulums are often used for questions about love, relationships, confidence and creativity. An amethyst weight will enhance guidance on life changes, spiritual matters and psychic energies. Pendulum weights can also be found made from lapis lazuli, obsidian, aquamarine and more. Do some more research into crystals and find out which one would be best for your purposes.

Quartz crystal is probably the most popular. It is especially good for dowsing for physical health issues and for clearly picking up different energy fields. Quartz is a fantastic conductor of energy, which is why it's used in clocks and watches to hold a specific frequency. The greater the material's conductivity, the clearer the message will be for the dowser.

Ideally, the end of the weight needs to be clearly pointed so the dowser can easily tell where it is pointing, especially when working with maps or divining charts (such as the ones on pages 150–157), to ensure the most exact information can be given. Some pendulums have a small hole in which to place a fragment of the material being looked for in the case of missing objects, or something from your lost pet, such as a clipping of their fur, to help with the search.

Now you've considered the materials it can be made from, the shape of the weight, and the type and length of the chain, you are ready to choose the perfect pendulum for you.

Choosing your pendulum

There are many factors to consider when choosing a pendulum, but mainly it needs to feel 'just right' to you. Tuning into what your intuition is telling you is one of the most important parts of dowsing – so why not start with the choosing of your pendulum?

Take your time when picking a pendulum for yourself. There's no rush and you want it to be the best one for you and your needs. You can buy them in esoteric shops, of which there are many in alternative towns such as Glastonbury or Totnes in the UK, but you can also find them online.

If purchasing in a shop, ideally, you want to be wearing comfortable clothing, have no heavy bags with you, and be alone with no time pressure at all.

TIPS FOR FINDING YOUR PERFECT PENDULUM

✳ Before entering the shop or starting the online search, take a deep breath in and exhale slowly, letting go of any negative thoughts or any preconceived ideas you may have about your pendulum. However, if you have a specific purpose in mind for your pendulum, such as dowsing for your health or finding the perfect new home, keep this in mind as you look.

✳ If the shop is busy, wait until it's quieter or move into an empty area with a few pendulums you like the look or feel of, to really tune into their energy in peace.

✳ You may want to close your eyes, take a few deep breaths and think of your purpose before opening your eyes and picking the first pendulum your eyes focus on.

✳ Next, sense how your body feels about it—excited, joyful or at peace? You may feel warmer with the one you like, or get a tingling sensation in your body. If you've looked at a few different pendulums, whether in a shop or searching online, are you strongly drawn to one in particular? Perhaps you love the colour, the shape or feel of it in your hand. Do you keep thinking about it, going back to it, really want to have it? That's your intuition telling you it's the right pendulum for you.

✳ If buying in a shop, spend time with the one to which you're most attracted. Does it feel comfortable when you hold the chain between your thumb and forefinger? Do you feel a sense of calm or happiness with it in your hand? Have a go at dowsing with it, ask if it's the right one for you (see page 44 for how). If you already have a pendulum but are looking for another one, dowse over the potential new one, or a selection, with the original. See which new one your pendulum picks for you.

When you find your perfect pendulum, because of its shape, colour, weight and feel, you now have a tool to help you pick up energy, expand your possibilities and help you understand yourself, and others, better. But first you need to prepare your pendulum by cleansing it, programming it and getting to know it. Let's get started!

Preparing to work with the pendulum

CLEANSING YOUR PENDULUM

Before starting to dowse with your pendulum, you need to cleanse it first. Whether it's been sitting in a shop for months, or in a drawer before being mailed out, it will have picked up energy from its surroundings. You don't want this to cloud its ability to give you the correct answer. Depending on what your pendulum is made from you can cleanse it in a variety of ways:

✳ Light a smudge stick, a small bundle of cleansing sage, and pass the pendulum through the smoke a few times.

✳ Leave it out under the full moon all night to allow its light to cleanse and recharge its energy - especially if it's is made from any quartz crystal. Do not leave it out in the sun however, as the heat can damage it or a cut crystal weight may even start a fire.

✳ Crystal pendulums can also be cleansed by burying in soil overnight and brushing it off gently in the morning.

✳ Briefly run it under pure or distilled water. Never use tap water, as this will add pollutants to it, or salt water, which will erode it over time. Leave it in a dark area to dry naturally, never in the sun as this could permanently change or damage it.

✳ If your pendulum is made from metal or wood, gently wipe it with a cotton cloth to take off any harmful energy it may have soaked up. Cleansing with water should be avoided.

Cleanse your pendulum regularly using one of these methods to re-energize it so it works at optimum level every time you need it.

STORING YOUR PENDULUM
Take care where you store your pendulum. Never store it anywhere near electronic gadgets as these emit electromagnetic frequencies that will be

soaked up by the pendulum and affect the way it works. Keeping your pendulum in a wooden or glass box is best as this will protect it from any harmful energy in the vicinity. Wrapped in a silk cloth or stored in a cotton bag will also protect it from scratches and any other external influences that might also affect how it works.

PREPARING YOURSELF

Get comfortable with your pendulum by carrying it around with you, in a small pouch or wrapped in a silk or organic cotton cloth, in your pocket for a few days. Take time to meditate with your pendulum. Just close your eyes, relax and let your mind clear as you feel the vibration from your pendulum when you hold it in your cupped palms. This will attune your energy to the pendulum and start the journey to working effectively with it in many areas of your life.

Set up a special area to work with it, if possible. Find an area in your home, free from distractions and any technological gadgets, where you will be able to sit calmly and quietly to use your pendulum. You could create a special corner for this, or perhaps you have a meditation altar that you can clear and prepare easily when you need to sit and dowse.

Spend some time sitting in this tranquil space every evening, by gentle candlelight, holding your pendulum by the chain, as described on pages 42–43. Without asking any questions or sensing any information, just allow your pendulum to move freely as you simply observe. This will help you get to know your pendulum so it becomes an extension of your subconscious mind.

Before you begin dowsing, spend time getting in touch with your subconscious mind, inner self, or centre. Sit comfortably in your quiet area, close your eyes and breathe deeply and calmly for a few minutes. Keep focusing on your breathing and let your mind clear itself of any superfluous thoughts. You may want to play some gentle music, with natural sounds, such as that used during Reiki sessions or massage treatments, for example.

Allow your body to relax until you feel a warmth running through it. Now focus your attention on your centre, where your stomach is, and let your awareness rest here. This is your connection to your inner self, where you feel your gut reactions, otherwise known as your intuition.

This is the part of you that pendulum dowsing connects with and amplifies the more you tune in to it. It is here that you will first receive the information the pendulum reveals.

Take some time before starting work with your pendulum to focus your mind and mentally prepare for the possible results it may bring. Let go of any preconceived ideas you may have about pendulum dowsing so you can be more receptive to the information it brings. Ask yourself if you are willing to be honest with whatever wisdom – or further questions – you receive. Stay open to the possibility of unusual or unexpected questions you find you need to ask your pendulum, and be neutral towards the answers or results – they may surprise you. Remember you are the mediator between the pendulum and the energy it picks up and transmits to you. Be open to receiving whatever presents itself and do not expect any particular outcome.

Holding the pendulum

There is great debate over which hand the pendulum should be held in. Some say it should be held in the hand you write with – known as your power hand – the right hand for most people. Others believe it should be the left hand, regardless of which is your dominant hand, as this connects you to your right brain, subconscious, your emotions and intuition. Try both to begin with and, chances are, one hand will allow the pendulum to oscillate more easily. Certainly, over time and with enough experience, you will come to know which hand is your 'pendulum hand'. Either way, you must hold the pendulum thread firmly, but in a relaxed way, between your thumb and index finger. The chain or string needs to be a certain length to allow the weight at the end to move freely. Certainly, while getting to know your pendulum, it's best to have the string length somewhere between 15–20 cm (7½–8 inches). This is the ideal length if you're working over a map or a chart, but if dowsing outside around 45 centimetres works well. Try out different lengths to find what's best for you, winding the rest of the chain around the length of your index finger or little finger, so it doesn't hang down and distract you. Ultimately, it should feel comfortable, like an extension of your arm.

When holding the pendulum in this way, don't prop your arm up on a table as this gives too little freedom for it to move. Instead, while seated or standing, push your elbow slightly into your body to support your lower arm which should be held at a right angle to the body, yet in a relaxed position.

Now you are ready to discover your pendulum's unique code – how it will express positive and negative answers to you when asked a question.

Discovering
yes and no

Now you are ready to work with your pendulum to determine how it will move when indicating its 'yes', 'no' and even 'maybe' answers. There are a number of ways you can do this as outlined on the following pages.

Usually pendulums move in a circular clockwise or ellipse motion for 'yes' and the same motion but in an anti-clockwise direction for 'no'. But your pendulum could also move in a variety of other ways: swing left to right; backwards and forwards away from your body and back towards it; in a diagonal movement; hang still or vibrate gently on its chain.

To find out your pendulum's individual code, start by taking a few calming, deep breaths to clear your mind and centre yourself. Sit comfortably, without crossing your legs so energy flows freely around your body. Hold your pendulum chain firmly but in a relaxed way between thumb and index finger, so it hangs freely. If you wish to do so, ask your higher consciousness or guides to help you receive the clearest answer for the highest good.

METHOD ONE: USING YOUR EMOTIONS TO PROGRAMME YOUR PENDULUM

Think of a happy event in your life, when you felt incredible joy. The pendulum will respond to your positive emotion by showing its movement for a positive answer – this is your 'yes'. You could draw the motion on a piece of plain paper if you like, so you remember it while you're first starting out.

Now think of a time in your life when you felt sad or disappointed. Watch how the motion of the pendulum changes. It might be the opposite to a 'yes' response, or it might be something different. But this is the movement your pendulum will make when the answer to a question is 'no'. Again, draw the shape of the movement on a piece of paper, if you wish.

Using the same technique, you can also get your pendulum to show you an 'ask again' response when the question you ask it isn't clear and perhaps needs formulating again, or the issue it's addressing goes deeper and more preliminary questions are needed first. Think of a time of confusion, when you got lost somewhere or weren't sure which job to take, for example. Whichever way the pendulum moves to this bewildered emotion is how it will move when you need to rephrase your question or try a different line of enquiry.

You can use this same technique to get your pendulum to show you its 'neutral' position – usually hanging still or maybe gently vibrating at the end of the string. Conjure up feelings of ambivalence, when you felt neither one way or the other about something. Watch how to pendulum moves – or, more likely, stays still.

METHOD TWO: ASK DIRECT YES / NO QUESTIONS

You may prefer to ask your pendulum to move to questions you know the answers to. So, ask it questions with an affirmative answer to get the 'yes' swing, such as: 'Do I live in London?' 'Am I xx years old?' 'Do I like dancing?' and see which way it moves. Then, to get the 'no' movement, ask questions that you know have a negative response, such as: 'Do I like bananas?', 'Do I have a brother?' and so on. Observe the movement it makes for a negative answer.

METHOD THREE: SHOW ME YES, NO AND MAYBE

Alternatively, you could simply ask your pendulum, politely, to 'show me a yes', and wait for it to move in a certain way. Then ask: 'show me a no', and see the change in movement that is to be the pendulum's 'no' answer to questions.

This way you can also ask your pendulum to 'show me a maybe', and 'show me a neutral' which could be a possible answer sometimes. See how all the movements differ, and note them down if you wish. Then proceed with asking it your own questions.

Until you establish a strong relationship with your pendulum, check the answers it gives to arbitrary questions first before you ask it more pertinent ones. Then you can be sure it's showing you its 'yes' or 'no' when needed.

Observe the size and clarity of the movements. In time, and with the right questioning, your pendulum will make bigger and smoother movements for stronger answers. So if it usually makes a clockwise circle for a 'yes' answer, if the response is 'most definitely YES!' you will see a larger and more obvious circle. If the pendulum makes much smaller or erratic moves, making you unsure of the response, it might be that you need to take a break, regain your calm, neutral state, or put the pendulum away and dowse another time.

Before any dowsing, always ask your pendulum if it is the right time to dowse. If a 'no' response is given, it may be that you need to clear your mind more. Take time to relax and focus on your breathing or visualise a cloudy sky, representing your murky mind, with the clouds slowly disappearing as your mind clears. Or perhaps other factors mean the question can't be answered right now, maybe things are still playing out so the outcome is unclear.

A pendulum's usual response can change over time. So, every now and then, or even before every dowsing session, just check in with your pendulum to make sure that it still giving you the same movement for 'yes', 'no' and 'maybe'.

Asking the right questions

You can ask your pendulum almost anything, from what to eat, where to go for a run, what to wear, study or purchase. Asking the right kinds of questions is crucial to the pendulum helping you with everything from relationship issues, health problems and spiritual path queries to revealing subconscious feelings and desires.

The way you formulate each question is very important – as the answer to each one has to be 'yes', 'no' or 'maybe'. So, don't put options in the question, such as, 'should I wear the red dress or the blue?', for example.

Always make the questions clear, direct and as simple as possible. Instead of saying something like, 'Might it be possible that this food could be the right thing to eat at some point?', say clearly, 'Should I eat this food now?' or 'Is this food good for me?' You don't want questions that could be answered several different ways depending on the interpretation. Remember to phrase your questions positively rather than negatively. Say or write your question: 'Is this friend good for me?' rather than, 'Is this person bad for me?' Don't formulate questions out of anger, jealousy or any other negative emotion. This is not the state with which to work with your pendulum.

Have a sense of ethics when you use a pendulum to ask questions. Don't ask questions just out of mere curiosity, only do it when you're actually interested in the response and it will help you in some way. Unless you're still practising working with your pendulum and still getting to know its responses, do not ask questions to which you already know the answer. Never ask the pendulum for the results of gambling bets, or ask it to reveal information about someone that may hurt them or be used to harm them in any way.

If your conundrum is complex, when several factors are involved in the answer, you may need to ask a few questions about the same subject to get a definite answer. Wanting to know the 'why' to a situation won't bring about reliable results from your pendulum, but ask the right questions and your pendulum will show you the right path to take.

Other than these factors, there are no rules about what you can ask your pendulum. It's more about how you form the question and with what intention.

Make sure you stop the pendulum moving completely after each time of answering.

As long as it's clear, simple and from a place of gaining genuine understanding and guidance, you can ask about any of the following subjects and more:

* Finding out more about yourself, your behaviour, talents, desires, likes, dislikes and hobbies

* Your professional abilities, ambitions, skills and career path

* Your relationships with others, whether professional colleagues, family, friends or intimate lovers

* Reasons for suffering—emotionally, mentally or physically

* Which alternative remedies, treatments or plants will help - but always consult your doctor if anything about your health worries you

* Food, nutrition and eating habits for optimum health

* Your environment, such as what area would be best to move to, what to plant in your garden, or how to remedy problems in

your surroundings such as electromagnetic stress or noisy
neighbours

* Chakra or meridian blockages

* Lost or missing objects or pets

* Searching for ghosts or finding out more about ancient legends
in mystical places.

Before you start – the three Ps

PURITY

It's best not to use your pendulum when stressed or tired as it will give inaccurate answers. Remember to ask, 'Is now a good time to dowse?' before any dowsing session. If the pendulum moves in the 'no' direction, or stays neutral, then put it away and try again another time, when you're feeling more rested and relaxed. The pendulum is not a toy and dowsing with it must be taken seriously. Make sure you are free of any intoxicants such as alcohol or even cigarette smoke as these will affect your mind, which needs to be completely neutral.

Remove any superfluous objects from your desk, table or surrounding area so you are not distracted by anything while dowsing. Turn off or put away any technological gadgets that emit electromagnetic frequency as this can influence your pendulum when you don't want it to. Take off any jewellery and your watch for the same reason. You want to omit anything that might have an effect, however small, on the pendulum's response.

POSTURE

Make sure your posture is upright, with your feet firmly on the ground, hip distance apart. This is so you can remain stable and comfortable in a position for a while. Don't cross your legs as this stops the energy flowing as freely as it should.

Take off any shoes as these insulate us from the earth; going barefoot will help you stay grounded throughout your dowsing session.

Place the hand not holding your pendulum on the table or resting in your lap – palm upwards – so that it doesn't affect the pendulum's movement in any way.

PROTECTION

If you are using your pendulum to ask questions on behalf of others, they may hold negative energies, such as fear or worry, which may transfer to you. Or, if you're dowsing in areas of strong energy such as old buildings or doing a bit of ghost hunting, then it's wise to protect yourself psychically.

You can easily do this by imagining yourself in a big ball of white light, or lighting a white candle in front of you while you work. Look into the light of the candle and ask for the protection of your guardian angels, spirit guides or other higher power. Trust that you are protected and ask for all the information you receive to be for the highest good.

If you direct all your questions to, and receive all perceptions from, your pendulum alone, any strong negative energies should be deflected anyway. Just be sure to cleanse your pendulum often and especially after such use as explained on pages 36–37.

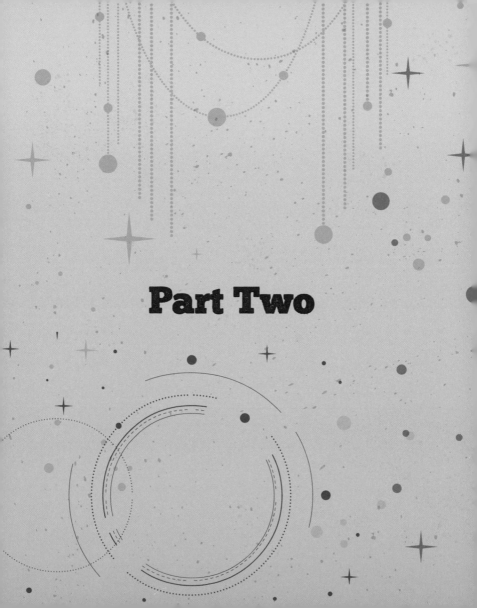

Part Two

PENDULUMS
IN
PRACTICE

Dowsing for decisions

When you're ready to ask your question, create an oasis of calm around yourself, wherever you are dowsing. Take your time to get fully centred in your body by taking some long deep breaths and dropping your awareness to your stomach. Clear your mind of extraneous clutter and fill it with what you would like a definitive answer on.

Think your question, or line of questioning, through clearly. You may want to write your questions down in a certain order, examining the bigger picture before narrowing down to the specifics. For example, if you're not sure what to study at college, first dowse to see if you should even carry on in formal education. Then ask if you should follow a vocational or academic course. Now you can ask your pendulum about which specific area to study, followed by the course and then the college you should attend.

Stay impartial to the results you get as they may not be what you wanted initially, and any preconceived ideas on the matter could cloud the response from your pendulum. Remain open to new questions arising out of unexpected outcomes.

Throughout the course of our lives, we have so many decisions to make. Some choices are easier to make than others, and all with varying consequences, from minor to completely life-changing. While you don't want to depend upon your pendulum for all decisions, dowsing with it can really help when you have a few possible paths to choose from and are unsure which one would be the best.

Always thank your pendulum for its guidance and assistance after working with it.

When you've checked it is the right time to dowse, and you've formulated your questions correctly, your pendulum will usually give a clear 'yes' or 'no' to help with the decision-making process. If it stays still or 'neutral', it may not have the answer yet, for whatever reason, so try again another time. Or perhaps your question may need re-phrasing; it needs to be answerable with a 'no' or a 'yes'. You can explicitly check if this is the case with the chart on page 150.

Be clear about your intention: are you asking the question for yourself or someone else; are you choosing something for the short or long term?

You can ask your pendulum for help with decisions such as:

* Which car to buy or where to go on holiday

* Finding a new home (more on pages 95-96)

* Deciding which quotation to go for if thinking of having work done on your home or garden

* Working out a course of study or change of career

Don't rely too much on your pendulum to make decisions for you. Continue to use your own intuition, wisdom and reason to work out what's best for you.

✳ Deciding who to go on a date with and where to go

✳ What to wear for a certain occasion

✳ Choosing between different crystals for healing or manifestation

✳ Whether to buy a certain item or choose between different ones

✳ If you should do something or not

If you're choosing between certain items in front of you, you can dowse over them and ask your question about their suitability. Try to narrow down your choices using your own instinct and reasoning first – you don't want to dowse over every car in the showroom!

CHOOSING A HOLIDAY

If you're trying to decide where to go on holiday, out of a couple of possible destinations, use your pendulum to help. Write your choices on pieces of paper, print out the details of those you like or use images from a brochure and then dowse over each one. Be clear about when you're going away and with whom, otherwise your pendulum might decide a tranquil spa holiday is right for you, which it may well be true for you, but you need to choose something a bit more active for all the family.

BUYING A CAR

Choosing a new car might take quite a few questions to work out which is the best one for you. Should it be new or second-hand, petrol or diesel, which make, style and size? Then you have to decide between those you go to see and test-drive. As with choosing a holiday, you can write the names of different cars you like on pieces of paper, place them on a clear table in front of you and dowse over each one asking 'is this right for me?'. When you've narrowed your decision down to two or three cars, you could write their individual registration numbers on slips of paper or visit the vehicles with your pendulum to dowse when in them, to see which car is the right one for you.

MAKING A CAREER DECISION

Deciding on a career path is probably one of the most important decisions you'll make. After all, it's what you'll spend most of your day doing, five or more days a week, for much of your life. You want it to be the right profession for you, something you enjoy and feel satisfaction doing, so that you are not just living for the weekends and longing to eventually retire.

Yet often, decisions about a new job or change of career are taken too lightly or just stumbled into. Perhaps you even feel that you're doing something because someone else – parents, teachers, or friends – suggested it would be good for you, but you wish you could do something else. You may be in a certain profession for reasons such as good income or nice colleagues even though you don't actually like the work itself, making every day a struggle. Or you may be happy with the job but work so hard you never have time to enjoy the fruits of your labour or see the people you care about most.

But what would you choose if you could make a change? What direction should you go in if just starting out? Should you relocate for a new job or stick with what you know? Whether you have a choice to make between two different job offers or have a more complex problem with your career, your pendulum can help you immensely.

Again, take time to think about the questions you need to ask. These could include:

∗ Should I leave this job?

∗ Would I be happy in the same profession?

∗ Would I be happy relocating?

* Do I want to work abroad?

* Do I want job A?

* Do I want job B?

* Do I want more money?

* Do I want fewer hours?

* Do I want a more creative position?

* Should I retrain in a different career?

You can then ask many questions to help you work out which career you should turn your attention to, honing in on your passions, interests and what you're good at. It may be that your pendulum encourages you to do more research, and then ask more questions at a later date. Keep going with your search until you feel happy in your heart, not just your rational mind, about your chosen path.

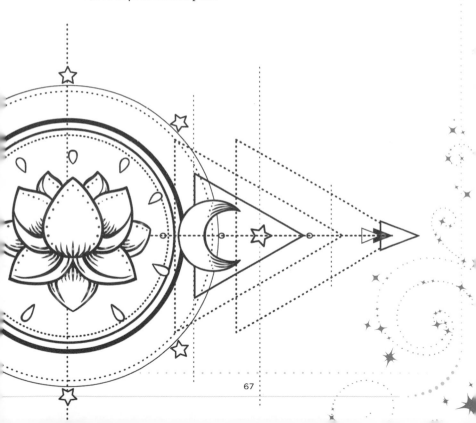

Relationship questions

Questions about relationships are some of the most popular that people put to the pendulum. There are so many issues at stake with matters of the heart, not only with intimate partnerships but with friends and family – and the pendulum comes in very handy to help.

However, it is one of the hardest lines of questioning in which to stay neutral, to ensure you get a clear answer. Take plenty of time before asking any relationship questions to really calm your mind, by sitting still and meditating for ten minutes or so beforehand. Breathe deeply and let go of any outcome.

Be sure to phrase your question clearly. Asking if so-and-so is the right person for you, depends on whether you want a long-term commitment or a date this weekend. Think hard about what sort of relationship you want. If you ask 'Will I marry this man or woman?' and the answer is 'no', you may decide to end the partnership if marriage is what you think you want. Yet it could have been a very happy, loving, lifelong commitment – just not involving a wedding.

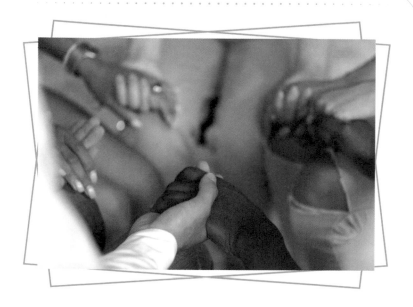

Even with friends, it might be that once a month quality time together is what you want or you might need to speak to someone every day – and this person isn't up for that. Different friendship styles can create confusion and discord so be prepared to discuss your feelings after dowsing if you want to build the friendship.

Ultimately, all relationships are about compatibility and this is something the pendulum can clearly reveal to you, when asked thoughtful and focused questions. You can simply ask your pendulum 'Am I compatible with so-and-so?' or 'Are these two people compatible?' if you're dowsing for someone else. Depending on the type of relationship you're dowsing about, you can then narrow down your connection to see if you are compatible emotionally, physically, mentally, spiritually, ethically or financially.

With a work relationship, or business partner, ethical and financial compatibility will be of prime concern. Whereas if you're looking for a housemate, your mutual attitude to finances will matter, but also whether you connect over things such as partying, cooking together and keeping the place tidy.

DOWSING FOR ROMANTIC RELATIONSHIPS

Sit quietly in your calm space and surround yourself with positive energies, perhaps by playing soothing music, lighting incense and candles or imagining white light all around you. As you're dowsing about matters of the heart, you could place some rose quartz, the crystal of love, self-esteem and romance, in front of you to imbue your dowsing session with loving energy towards yourself.

Remember to keep your mind free from any attachment to an outcome, let your pendulum show you the way forward. First, ask if it is the right time to dowse. If it is, take some time to picture the person or people you are asking questions about. Then ask away.

HELPING OTHERS WITH THEIR RELATIONSHIP QUESTIONS

If you are dowsing on romantic relationships for someone else, there are a couple of factors you need to clarify first.

If they look upon pendulum dowsing as a bit of a joke, they may ask flippant questions. You will lose the connection you have with your pendulum and results won't be accurate. It's not something to do as a game with a group of friends, much better one-to-one with someone with serious intentions for good guidance. Then you can work with them to formulate specific questions that get to the heart of the matter.

If they have intense emotions about the situation, this may cloud the pendulum's response. Either ask them to try and calm their emotions, in the same way you do, or ask their questions of your pendulum when they are not around.

After preparing your calm, centred self, as described above, either imagine both people involved in the issue, or write their names on pieces of paper. Place the papers on a clutter-free table in front of you, maybe surrounded by your rose quartz crystals. If it's the right time to dowse according to your pendulum, hold it in the usual way over the pieces of paper, in turn, as necessary, and ask your questions.

DOWSING FOR OTHER RELATIONSHIPS

Family arguments may be able to be resolved with the help of a pendulum. If you feel that an issue keeps coming up again and again, such as blame for past wrongs or unfairness in your upbringing, you can ask your pendulum if a problem is caused by this or that factor. Then, remembering to ask questions with a 'yes' or 'no' answer, you can determine what might help resolve matters, such as counselling, some time apart or a big hug.

Friendships can be fraught with difficulties and change over time. If things are going wrong, it can create as much heartache and unhappiness as any other relationship breakdown. But you don't have to stick with a friend out of guilt or just because you've known each other since you were babies, especially if you feel sad, fed up or angry. Asking the right questions of your pendulum about a friendship can bring clarity about the energies involved and help you make a decision on how best to move forward.

Choosing people to live with can be a complicated decision – and go horribly wrong quite quickly with incompatible people. It all depends how long you intend to live with someone for – a year at university in a rented flat or will you be buying a house together to live in for the longer-term?

If many people are involved, write everyone's names – including your own or the questioner's – on separate pieces of paper. Place all these on a clear area in front of you before calming your mind and preparing to dowse in the usual way. Place yourself or the questioner in the centre surrounded by the others in a circle. Focusing on your question, for

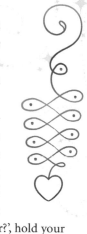

example 'is this person compatible to live with me for a year?', hold your pendulum over one of the names and note down the response, including how strong the movement is. Move on to each name, asking the same question and noting down the details afterwards. If you are trying to narrow down a list of names you can do so picking those with the strongest response, and even regrouping those and asking further direct questions about your compatibility with them.

The same method above can also be used to choose **business partners or colleagues** to work with in a team or on a certain project. Again, you need to work out the nature and length of the business or project. All those involved need to be thinking along the same lines, but again compatibility of work ethic, financial know-how, or creativity is key in work relationships too.

Health

Dowsing to improve your health is one of the most rewarding ways to use the pendulum, both instantly and over the longer term. You can dowse over different foods to reveal their freshness and help decide which is better for you to eat. Your pendulum can enable you to find the best vitamin supplements to take, ease addictions and choose alternative remedies for ailments. It can even help soothe pain and rebalance your chakra system to bring about optimum vitality.

FOOD

We are what we eat, or so the experts say, and it pays to eat a good balance of the best nutrients for us to keep our body and mind in top condition. But what are the right foods for us? They might not be the ones you like the most. And you could be missing out on vital nutrients by avoiding foods you think you shouldn't eat, for example, those that are high in fat but are very nutritious, such as avocado or nuts.

By working with your pendulum you can find out the best foods and drinks for you. Start with the diet you usually eat. Either line up the actual ingredients you eat on a daily basis and dowse over each one in turn, asking if they are good for you to eat at this current time. Or you can write the foods on separate slips of paper and dowse over those in the same way. You can ask your questions of general food groups – for example, bread, nuts or meat – or specific varieties or brands of food, such as a choice between certain types of cereals or vegetables.

As with all dowsing, the more vigorous the answer the more you should or shouldn't eat that food. However, don't restrict your diet so much that you're not eating a good variety of nutrients. Always remember that most foods are fine in moderation and a little of what you fancy does you good, as the old saying goes. Unless you have an allergy to something, of course, and then you need to get this checked out by a doctor.

If this is an issue for you, the pendulum can also help you get to the bottom of what it is to which you're allergic or intolerant. You may think you are allergic to all dairy, for example, but by asking the pendulum about different types of dairy products, you may discover that you can, after all, eat kefir yogurt, for its promotion of healthy gut bacteria.

In the supermarkets it can be hard to tell which foods are the freshest or completely chemical-free. If you're brave enough, you could take your pendulum shopping with you and dowse over your choices to find out which ingredients have the most vitality and health-giving energy at that moment. But don't fall into a habit of dowsing over everything you eat. Find out what's best for you and then relax and enjoy eating a healthy balanced diet.

SUPPLEMENTS

Many of us supplement our diets with extra vitamins, minerals and herbal remedies. But are they actually doing us any good? Could they be reacting badly with other medicines we're taking? And might they just be a big expense for no real benefit? Again, your pendulum can help you to work out if a supplement is worth taking or not.

If you already have a certain vitamin or supplement, you can dowse over the bottle of

tablets and ask your questions to find out if it is the right one for you right now. Remember to be direct with your question. Asking 'Is it ok for me to take this supplement?' might get a favourable answer because it's not doing you any harm. But, 'Is this supplement doing me good?' factors in whether it's actually benefitting your health or just costing you money.

If you are concerned about lacking certain vitamins or minerals in your diet, you can ask your pendulum to check if you have a nutrient deficiency by saying, for example, 'Do I need to take a supplement of iron?'. Again, in the health food shop, choosing between different brands of supplements, you can ask your pendulum which would be the best ones for you. Or, if you'd rather dowse at home, list a few exact names of supplements on pieces of paper and dowse over each one asking if it would be the right match for you.

Use your pendulum to also discover if a combination of different supplements is good for you. Many people take a few different vitamins and minerals every day, but some might not combine well or might even cancel each other out. Ask if you would be better off leaving one (or more) of your vitamins out of the mix, by dowsing over each one separately. If you get a "no" answer over one, or more, then they can be left out.

You may be worried about a prescription medicine you're taking, and can also dowse over that asking if it is the right one for you, or ask specific questions about your concerns over the tablets. **But never, ever stop taking any prescribed medication without consulting your doctor first.** Any worries you have over your prescription need to be discussed with your medical practitioner straight away.

BACH FLOWER REMEDIES

Bach Flower Remedies were discovered and made using dowsing. Their creator Dr. Arthur Bailey was treated for a post-viral illness by the wife of his homeopathic doctor who used dowsing to discover the right remedies for him. When he was well, Dr. Bailey dowsed around his garden to find flowers with healing properties. He came up with about 20 new remedies using this method over the next decade or so, and now there are hundreds of different Bach Flower Remedies to choose from.

How to use: After researching the various flower remedies that might work for your condition, be it trauma, depression or anxiety, you can dowse out of a selection for the right one for you. Place the best ones according to what you've learned in a circle, with the labels facing away from you. Hold your pendulum over the top of each one and it will respond positively or negatively, helping you narrow down which remedy or remedies to use.

HELP WITH ADDICTIONS

* As well as helping with allergies and ailments, your pendulum can also ease addictions to substances including alcohol and cigarettes. Over time, careful questioning of the pendulum could lead to the heart of why you crave a certain substance.

* When you feel a strong desire to binge drink, eat all the biscuits in the house or smoke yet another cigarette, take some time out with your pendulum instead.

* As usual, sit quietly, calming yourself with a few deep breaths as you (try to) empty your mind of powerful thoughts of that which you intensely desire.

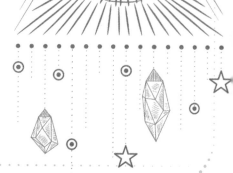

* Question these cravings and get to the bottom of what they are really about. Is it to mask a feeling of loneliness, boredom or inadequacy perhaps? From where and when in your past do these feelings come?

79

* Be honest and get deep in your enquiry. But be gentle with yourself, this is not about finding fault but helping you get healthier in mind, body and spirit.

* Write down on pieces of paper any questions that arise or options the pendulum could answer 'yes' or 'no' to when held over them.

* Pausing to simply calm down and question why you have this craving, journalling any realisations about your addiction, and taking time for yourself, will hopefully reduce the overwhelming desire or feeling of panic you get when you can't have something you crave.

* You might find you go longer between cigarettes or gradually decrease the amount you drink, perhaps substituting your craving with something healthier or a more self-loving activity.

Over time, you can fully examine the reasons that you are addicted to certain substances, learn a lot about your deeper self and regain control over your mind and body, boosting your overall health and wellbeing – all through using your pendulum.

Healing

Not only can your pendulum give you answers to questions and help guide you towards what's best for you, it can also encourage healing by unwinding pain and balancing energy. With pendulum healing, you can ask your dowsing tool to remove negativity, trauma or pain from something or fill it with positive energy. You can also send healing vibes to your pets, someone far away, or work on unblocking a person's chakras leading them to better health and wellbeing.

You can use your regular dowsing pendulum, but cleanse it before and after you do any healing with it. Alternatively, you could get a pendulum specifically for healing, with the weight depicting a healing symbol, such as the tree of life or the merkaba, or made from a specific crystal for healing, such as clear or rose quartz, aquamarine, carnelian or hematite, for example.

REMOVING PAIN

To work with a pendulum for healing you simply hold it as usual, loosely but firmly between index finger and thumb, over an affected area, and it will begin spinning and working its magic. Try holding it over a friend or someone who needs help with an ailment as they sit or stand in front of you. Simply hold your pendulum over the top of their head and allow its healing powers to enter their aura via their crown chakra (see pages

85–91 to learn more about chakras and where they are located in the body).

Or you can command your pendulum to perform specific healing tasks by asking it, politely, to release any trauma from your cells, or soreness from an injury and to increase your vitality, happiness, consciousness or love to the highest possible level.

Let's say you've got aching feet from walking around all day and you want to use your pendulum to soothe them. Sit comfortably and hold your pendulum over one foot at a time. As it starts to spin round, say, 'Please remove the pain from this injury'. Let your pendulum keep spinning around until it starts to change its movement, usually moving from side to side, indicating that the healing is complete. Do the same with your other foot.

You can do a similar healing on your pets as they lie in their bed. Simply hold the pendulum over them and ask it to heal any wounds or increase life force in your beloved animal. The pendulum will spin around to send healing energy to your pet, and either stop or swing back and forth when it is done.

If any pain is temporary, the pendulum might spin fast or wildly at first and then come to a stop quite swiftly. However, if it's more of a deep-rooted problem, your pendulum may take a lot longer to reach stillness.

You can use your pendulum to help with all sorts of physical, emotional and spiritual conditions – but always consult your doctor if worried. Long-term pain can be a warning sign for something more serious, so don't just keep removing the pain, either with your pendulum or with painkillers.

> Always remember to cleanse your pendulum before and after any healing session.

SCANNING THE BODY

If you're unsure about where the pain is really coming from, you can use your pendulum to scan your body, or someone else's, to find the problem area. In France especially, where pendulum use in medicine is more common, many chiropractors and doctors use a dowsing pendulum to narrow down areas of pain on the spine or other parts of the body.

When working with energy in this way, you could be open to a lot of negativity, so make extra sure you calm and ground yourself, surround your body with protective light and keep your intentions very clear. Ensure your questions are simple and direct; ask your pendulum to help you locate the source of the problem. Focus on your breathing and the sensations in your body.

BALANCING THE CHAKRAS

Hold your pendulum to one side of your body, and bring yourself into your calm, centred state. Ask the pendulum to help you balance your chakras. Focus your mind on each part of your spine as you move upwards or move the palm of your free hand to rest slightly in front of – but not touching – each chakra. Travel from your root chakra at the base of your spine, up through all the chakras to the crown chakra at the top of your head (see pages 89–91 for exactly where the chakras are located). Stop at each chakra and see how the pendulum reacts. It will stay in its neutral position unless it finds negative energy in a certain area, and then it will start to move in some way to release that energy and bring you some relief. Let the pendulum move in whatever way and for however long it needs

to, until it comes back to its resting or neutral state. Then carry on moving very slowly up the chakra line, watching for any movement if and when it hits negative energy again.

If you suffer from a particular problem in one of the chakras, such as headaches or sore throat, ask the pendulum to help with this and work on that area until it eases. But don't overwork one particular chakra as this will imbalance the others, and the system works as a whole.

If working on another person, you can do exactly the same with them. As they lay down in front of you or sit with their arms by their side, move your pendulum slowly up the centre line of their body, and watch for any movement at any point along the chakras. Allow whatever movement needs to take place to bring relief. Wait for the pendulum to stop and then move on slowly up the body, finishing at the crown.

When you've finished balancing the chakras, especially if there was a blockage in any of the upper areas, it's quite common to feel dizzy or light-headed. Take some time to sit quietly and drink some water to help you feel more grounded.

Remember to cleanse the pendulum thoroughly after any chakra balancing session as it will have taken on negative energy and you don't want that transferring between people. See pages 36–37 for how to cleanse your pendulum.

The chakras

According to ancient Indian Sanskrit texts the chakras are centres of swirling energy that sit at points along the length of the body, from the base of the spine to the crown of the head. They distribute life force – or *prana* – through the body keeping it balanced, changing and growing in a healthy way.

Daily life, with its stress, drama and trauma, can cloud these energy vortexes and make areas of our life unbalanced, leading to mental or physical illness. Our whole body, emotions and spirit are interlinked and

when one aspect is affected it can contribute to ill health in another area. For example, decreased mobility due to back pain can lead to depression, and long-term depression can lead to further illness such as heart disease. We need to treat the whole system to improve our health – and the chakras are part of this.

The seven major chakras

1st
Root chakra: red — base of the spine

Connected to our physical energy, health and ability to be grounded. If blocked you may feel insecurity more deeply, as well as frustration and anxiety. Manifests in problems with feet and legs, osteo-arthritis, bowel trouble and chronic long-term illness.

2nd
Sacral chakra: orange — about an inch below the naval

Balances emotions, sexuality and desire with self-worth, intuition and creativity. If this chakra is clogged you might have more emotional outbursts than usual, feel isolated and lack vitality. Physically, blockage here can result in lower back pain, impotence, and kidney, prostrate or uterus issues.

3rd

Solar plexus chakra: yellow — centre of the body just below the breastbone and shoulder blades

All about personal power, confidence, ambition and drive. When balanced, it brings joy and sharp intellectual focus, imbalanced it leads to anger, addiction and low self-esteem. Physically, it links to the central nervous system so can create worry and over-sensitivity if blocked and lead to stomach problems such as ulcers or digestive issues, diabetes, allergies and chronic fatigue.

4th

Heart chakra: green or pink — centre of chest

Related to love, compassion and kindness. If this chakra is imbalanced you might feel sorry for yourself, paranoid or indecisive. Problems with the arms, hands or fingers might manifest if blocked long-term, or illnesses associated with the heart and lungs, such as heart disease, high blood pressure or asthma.

5th

Throat chakra: blue — at the throat area of the neck, just below the collar bone

Linked to the voice and clear speech, when balanced this chakra promotes creative self-expression and communication. Out of balance, you can experience blocked creativity and reluctance to speak up or share your emotions. Any illness to do with the throat, ears or thyroid stems from imbalance here.

6th
Third eye chakra: indigo — between the eyebrows

A clear third eye chakra means strong intuition, psychic ability and altruism. Weakened, it can make you feel either unassertive or egotistical, and afraid of doing well in the world. Headaches, nightmares, eye problems or neurological issues may manifest if this area is blocked.

7th
Crown chakra: violet or crystal clear — just above the top of the head

Connected to spiritual wisdom, spirit guides and enlightenment. When imbalanced you may feel confused, frustrated or depressed. Physical manifestations of imbalance here include epilepsy, exhaustion and depletion due to environmental pollution.

There are other minor chakras located in others areas of the body, including the soles of the feet, palms of the hands, in front of the ear and behind the eyes. When scanning over the body with your pendulum, you could also include these areas or watch for the pendulum to pull in a direction other than down the central line of the body.

MORE PENDULUM HEALING

✳ An easy way to bring about healing is to allow your pendulum to fill you with nature's energy. If you're feeling tired or stressed, find a field, tree or another beautiful spot in nature to stand in. Taking a few deep breaths to bring calm to your being, focus on what you need—relief from pain, anxiety or depression. Now, holding your pendulum, turn slowly around in a circle until you feel energy moving into you from your natural surroundings. This could feel like a tingling or warm sensation in the hand and arm holding your pendulum, or an overall raising of your energy and boost to your mood.

✳ You can also ask your pendulum to infuse anything—such as food or drink, for example—with positive energy. Clear your mind and imagine yourself in a big ball of loving, upbeat, joyful energy. Focus on the object while asking your pendulum to fill it with positivity or increase its vitality. Your pendulum will move as it does this; let it carry on until it comes to a natural stop. Once it has stopped, it is a sign that the object is now filled with positive energy.

SENDING HEALING TO OTHERS

You can use your pendulum to send healing energy to anyone who needs it but who lives far away, or to friends or family that you are estranged from to try and heal the relationship.

Sit in your quiet area and calm your thoughts by taking some deep, relaxing breaths. Choose a certain coloured candle to light to send different kinds of energy. You can pick white for healing, green for lovers, pink for children, animals, friends and reconciliation, blue for travellers or anyone with career troubles, brown for the elderly or yellow for anyone needing help with their studies or exams.

Hold a crystal pendulum in front of the lighted candle. Gently spin your pendulum so the light from the candle reflects through it. Look into the spiralling light and project the person you are sending energy to into the pendulum. Say out loud or think what you would like this person to know and imagine them receiving your words with happiness.

Keep spinning your pendulum even faster, so the colours become a blur. When it reverses spontaneously, blow out the candle and send that light and loving intention to the person you've been thinking about. Even if you feel negatively towards someone, sending them positive energy through your pendulum in this way may help the relationship heal.

Home

Y our pendulum can come in very handy around the home, helping you make decisions about decorating, DIY and hiring help. And if you're looking to move house or relocate entirely, use your pendulum to focus your search and find the right place for you without worry.

FINDING A NEW HOME

When you're looking for a new place to live – whether renting or buying – you can use your pendulum to help you decide where to move to. Once you've rationally narrowed down your search to between two or three ideal places, or countries if moving further afield, enlist your pendulum to help make the final decision.

You can dowse over an outspread map, or the names of the places written on separate pieces of paper, set out on a completely bare table in front of you. You don't want anything influencing the pendulum, such as souvenirs or flyers from a certain area.

Calm your mind and focus on your questions, remembering to keep them clear and direct. Asking if a certain area is right for you in the immediate future is probably best, or if you have a time-frame in mind, state that.

Once you've finalised the best area to move to, you can then use your pendulum to choose between certain properties in that locale. Again, dowse over the addresses written on pieces of paper, or if you've chosen a few houses from an estate agents, you can dowse over the printed out details. Clear your mind of any emotional attachment towards the result. The pendulum will be picking up if each property has the right energy for you, regardless of which one you think might suit you best, be closer to transport or have the nicest garden.

You can also ask your pendulum about the finer details of each property, such as the price, structure of the building, or the timing of the move. Take your time thinking about what you really need to know about your new home, and then ask simple questions that can be answered with a 'yes' or a 'no'.

When viewing homes you can take your pendulum with you and dowse directly in the property to discover if the energy there is right for you or whether certain issues like shared access or a spot of damp are deal-breakers.

AROUND THE HOME

There's nothing worse than repainting or recarpeting a whole room and then feeling like it could have been a few shades lighter. Ask your pendulum to help you choose new furniture, carpets or the perfect colour to redecorate your place with, and you could save yourself a costly mistake. Either take it to the showrooms with you and discreetly dowse over your favourites, or borrow sample colours or designs and ask your pendulum questions about them at home.

HIRING HELP

If you need to pay professionals to do the decorating, building work, cleaning or gardening, ask your pendulum who best to hire. Get a few different business cards or leaflets and dowse over them to see if you should get quotes from them. Then, when you have a few quotes, dowse over each one to discover which would be the best option for you. It might not just be a case of choosing the cheapest. Ask questions such as 'Is this company reliable/trustworthy/ecologically sound/ethical?' 'Will I be happy having them working in my home?' and 'Is this the right company/person to complete this particular project?' and so on.

REARRANGING

Sometimes a room in your home might not feel quite right and your pendulum can help you work out why. Perhaps the energy in your office doesn't feel very inspiring, you find it hard to get to sleep in your bedroom, or the furniture arrangement in your living room feels crowded or chaotic.

Start by dowsing in every room in your home, asking your pendulum if the energy is positive in each area. If the pendulum gives a negative response, you could ask questions to find out why, such as 'Is it because of the décor/clutter/layout/furniture?'.

When you have the areas and issues you need to work on, clear out any clutter first of all. Think about how best to rearrange furniture to help energy flow better and so that the room does not feel so cramped. You might want to work with Feng Shui ideas to enhance the energy in certain areas with crystals, plants or specific ornaments. You can always move things around and check in with your pendulum if the energy flow is better, but you should be able to feel it improve almost immediately.

If you're unsure which bedroom would make the best office, or where to have the kids' playroom, for example, ask your pendulum in each of the rooms you have in mind, or make a plan of your house and dowse over the rooms on that.

DIY PROBLEMS

Your pendulum can help you detect and rectify problems around the home, such as finding a leak or an electrical fault somewhere. Beware of using a metal pendulum near live wires though – that could be very dangerous!

But, if your vacuum cleaner has stopped working, for example, it might not be an irreparable problem but simply a blown fuse. And you might have been all for throwing it out completely! If part of a stereo system breaks the whole thing stops working and it can be costly to get it all looked at by an expert. But you can methodically hold your pendulum over different parts of it and ask if the problem lies there. This way you can get to the bottom of any issues at home without making any expensive mistakes through lack of information.

Garden

From planning your perfect garden to picking which pot plants to grow indoors, your pendulum can really help with growing your own green space.

As plants are part of our natural environment, pendulums can easily pick up whether they are happy and healthy where they are situated, or

whether they would benefit from being moved to another position. If you have a poorly plant, dowse over it asking questions such as 'Are you happy in this position?', 'Do you need more/less watering?', 'Would you like some more nutrients?' and ask which nutrients it might need – you can write them down and dowse over them. Maybe it just needs repotting into a larger pot or pruning to stay healthy. You can ask your pendulum all of these questions and it will show you the way to help your plant grow better, whether in your home or in the garden.

If a plant doesn't like where it is, ask which area it would like to be moved to, for example, 'Would you prefer to be in the southern corner of the room or garden?', 'would you like more shade/more sunlight/to be near the window/under the tree?' If it's outside, you can walk slowly around your garden with your pendulum and ask it to show you a clear 'yes' in the place the plant would most like to be. Do the same with a houseplant to find its optimum location indoors.

CREATING AN OUTSIDE SPACE

Perhaps you're planning your garden from scratch – again your pendulum can be a great help. But before you start dowsing, check the basics of your garden's aspect through your own observations:

* Which direction does your garden face?

* Where does it get most sun?

* Where is it always in shade?

* Where does the sun move to throughout the day?

Find out what type of soil you have, whether chalky or clay, acidic or alkaline, as this will determine what grows best there. You can use images online to check your soil against, or simply ask your pendulum – remember the answer needs to be 'yes' or 'no'. Dowse over the soil to find out if any nutrients need to be added, such as fertilizer, to help plants grow well.

Think about what you want to use your outside space for – growing fruit or vegetables, having somewhere for the children to play, or a place to sit in the sun and relax. You can ask your pendulum which area(s) would be best for the purpose you have in mind, either by dowsing around the garden itself or by writing your ideas on separate pieces of paper, laying them out on a clean table in front of you and dowsing over each one.

Once you've decided upon the different areas in your garden, use your pendulum to help you choose which plants to purchase, and where best to position them. Do some research into which plants would suit

TEST YOUR PENDULUM'S POWER WITH PLANTS

The most successful gardeners are usually intuitive.
As pendulum dowsing is part of your intuitive skills,
try this test to help you with your plants.

1   At the garden centre, randomly pick three unfamiliar flowers or plants without reading the labels.

2   Ask your pendulum to choose one for you — it will either pull towards one as you hold your pendulum above them all in a row, or show you a positive response when you hold it over each one. It may not be the most healthy-looking plant, but it is right for you on another level. Do not read the label.

3   When at home with your plant, ask your pendulum to choose the best place to plant it: is it best in full sun, in the shade, in rich compost or stony soil? If you don't have a garden, but still want to do this test, use three pots of window boxes with different soil compositions in, facing different directions.

4   Plant your flower, herb or plant in the area chosen by the pendulum, with the intention that it's linked to you positively.

5   Ask the pendulum how much water your plant needs, by setting up containers of water and dowsing over them. Similarly, ask what time of day would be best to water your growing greenery.

6   As your plant thrives, you will know that your pendulum's choice was right and sticking to it and all other guidance you dowsed for was crucial to your plant's wellbeing.

How empowering to know your pendulum was spot on!

your soil and space before writing down your preferences on pieces of paper and dowsing over each one to discover which would work well in the places you have in mind.

Then, when you go to the garden centre, you can dowse over individual plants to find out if they are healthy before you buy them. You can check whether they would thrive in the area you have in mind and discover if they need extras such as plant food or support canes.

Before you start digging a hole in your garden in which to put your plant, dowse to be sure it's the perfect place.

1   Stand in the centre of your garden and slowly turn in a circle while holding your pendulum.

2 Ask your dowsing tool to show you the right direction by pulling towards a certain area or showing you its 'yes' movement.

3 Then go to that section of the garden and ask again, to find a more specific spot, such as against the fence or at the front of the border, for example.

4 Alternatively, if you have drawn a plan of your garden, you can simply dowse over that to see when your pendulum gives you a positive response over a certain area.

Even when you've planted up, you can still ask your pendulum to tell you if and when to feed your plant, when to prune it back or to split the plant into more than one. Use the ideas at the start of this section if your plant is looking less than healthy. Your pendulum will help you get to the bottom of the problem so your plants can grow well again.

GROWING FOR GOOD HEALTH

If you fancy growing food to cook or herbs to improve your health, again your pendulum can help you decide which varieties would be best for you and the space you have to grow them in. The choice can be overwhelming, so dowsing can help you to decide.

* First, have a good think about whether you want to grow staple foods or treats that can be expensive to buy in the shops but fairly easy to grow at home, such as berries or salad leaves.

* Do you want your crops to feed your family, be gourmet ingredients, or healing herbs for homemade teas or oils?

* How much time have you got to tend to your crops or would you rather they were a bit easier to look after?

* Will you be growing organic produce, without the use of pesticides? It's much better for you and the planet to grow chemical-free crops, but it means you'll need hardy varieties and have to keep an eye out for pests.

* How much space have you got for food plants; what works best in that area and with your soil?

When you've worked it all out, use your pendulum as with all plants to help you choose the right variety, the most healthy plants, whether to go for seeds or seedlings, and decide how many to plant and exactly where.

When to plant crops is also an important question to ask your pendulum. Each food has a particular growing and harvesting season that you must get right. It's not always the spring when everything starts growing. Depending on what you're planting you may have to bed it in during the autumn or winter for crops the following year. Biodynamic farming is a method of planting and harvesting according to the cycles of the moon and can be highly beneficial for fruit, vegetables and herbs. Read up on the growing cycles of the foodstuffs you want, and ask your pendulum to guide you on the perfect time to plant, and pick, your produce.

Finding things

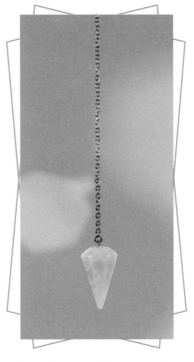

Your pendulum can help if you've mislaid something important to you, whether that's your door keys, jewellery or paperwork. You can enlist its help to find lost pets, and even missing people – although this comes with such intense emotion that it is definitely better left to the professionals. Much like dowsing enables people to find underground sources of water or minerals, you can also use your pendulum to locate archeological finds and fossils buried in the soil. Whatever you're looking for, ask your pendulum to help.

LOST OBJECTS

When you know you last had the car key in your kitchen, or that you must have lost those sapphire earrings in the bedroom, dowsing for them can be much like the hot and cold game you might have played as a child.

Before you begin though, you need to focus on exactly what it is you're looking for. So, imagine those special earrings in as much detail as you can, or think about which car you need the keys for and what the keyring attached to them looks like. Then, state out loud that your intention is to find this specific item or items.

Now, holding your pendulum as usual, take a few deep breaths and start asking it questions to find your missing item. 'Are my sapphire earrings in my bedroom?' If 'yes' you can move to that room and start narrowing down your search to specific areas of that room, for example, 'Are the sapphire earrings behind the bed/in a drawer/behind the mirror...?' Or you can walk slowly around the room and ask your pendulum to show you when you are getting close to the objects you're looking for. The 'yes' response should get clearer as you get closer to the item.

SEARCHING WITH A DIRECTIONS CHART

If you need to search a larger area, say you've lost your keys outside somewhere in your town, or your cat has gone missing, you may need to use a different method involving the direction chart on page 151 and a compass.

If you have a larger pendulum and the chart in the book is too small, photocopy it at a larger size in order to see clearly which way your pendulum is swinging.

As before, take some time to picture what you're looking for in your mind's eye. With a missing pet, remember their sound, smell, how they make you feel, or any memories you have connected to them. You may want to look at a photo of them, or touch their bed. If you have their lead or collar, you could hold that in your other hand as you hold your pendulum in your usual hand. This is to establish a strong telepathic connection between you and your missing animal, that the pendulum can pick up and to which it can respond.

Next, use a compass to line up magnetic north with the north on your chart. Hold your pendulum at the central cross where the north/south axis meets the east/west one.

State very clearly, and in as much detail as you can, what you want your pendulum to help you to find. Ask it to take you to your beloved animal, rather than to where your pet is at the time of asking the question – otherwise you could end up chasing it around!

Now, ask your pendulum which direction you should go in to start your search. Begin over the north direction on the chart and then move your pendulum slowly, clockwise, around the circle, above all the directions. You will either feel a pull down to that direction on the chart, or see your pendulum's usual positive response, for the right direction to go in.

Move off in that direction, still holding your chart and pendulum, watching for the pendulum's positive movement to slow down or stop. When its response changes, stop walking and realign your chart's north with that of your compass – you may need to put the chart down on a flat surface to do this. Line your pendulum up with the central axis again and ask which direction you need to go in next to carry on your search.

Keep following this method as best you can despite obstacles such as stairs or hedgerows, all the while watching your pendulum's movements. As you get closer to the object or animal in question your pendulum's movements should become strong and more pronounced so you know you are in the right location.

If looking for a lost pet, call out their name, be patient and look in less obvious hiding places. Cats especially can squeeze into all sorts of spots and may well be asleep. If the pendulum has indicated that your pet is in a certain location, look and listen carefully for signs there.

If necessary, you could also use this method using maps over a wider area gradually narrowing down your search to a map of a smaller locale before going out into the actual spot to search. Always place your map fully unfolded and on a flat, clutter-free surface with no distractions. Again, focus clearly on what you want to find before asking your pendulum to lead you there.

ANCIENT ARTEFACTS AND FOSSILS

As dowsing began all those centuries ago with the search for underground water, it's not hard to believe your pendulum can help you find other buried treasures. Many archeologists have successfully dowsed to locate hidden ancient ruins, such as Roman baths, Bronze Age artefacts or coins from various bygone eras. And you can do the same, either by dowsing over a map or directly in an area you have permission to explore.

Previously, you've asked your pendulum to help you find something specific, whereas with archeology you're asking it to help you find something of historical value while you may not know exactly what that thing is. So, after asking if it is a good time to dowse about this subject first, ask your pendulum where the best place is to start your search or to dig a trench to begin looking for fossils and other exciting finds.

However, it's not a good idea to start digging up a stranger's field simply because your pendulum pointed you in that direction. Much better to get in touch with the British Society of Dowsers' archeological dowsing group for local workshops or events where you can look for artefacts or go on properly organised archeological digs with groups of other like-minded dowsers.

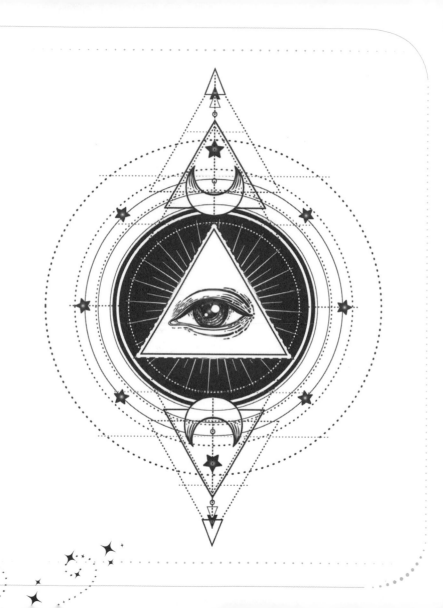

Picking up energies

P endulum dowsing is a particularly good way to pick up the different energies surrounding us all the time that we might not be able to see or feel. These invisible energies, such as electro-magnetic frequency (EMF) or ley lines, can have a powerful effect on us mentally, emotionally, spiritually and of course physically, without us realising.

Some people are more sensitive to these energies than others, and they can have positive or negative effects. For example, at the centre of ancient standing stone circles, your pendulum can reveal very powerful energy which can connect us to the land and our heritage. On the other hand, EMFs can make you feel constantly tired or unwell, and you can use your pendulum to get to the root of the problem and remedy it.

ELECTRO-MAGNETIC FREQUENCY (EMF)

Modern technology emits certain electro-magnetic radiation waves, which many people are sensitive to and find it can give them headaches, insomnia, fatigue and worse. Nowadays, we're surrounded by mobile phones, computers and wifi routers, so it might be helpful to know which, in particular, is causing you the most problems.

You can dowse to find out if it's your specific mobile phone that's giving you headaches or all smart phones, in which case, never put your phone directly up to your ear. Talk on speakerphone or use earphones instead, and turn your phone onto aeroplane mode when not in use. This stops it trying to find a signal and pulsing out energy that can negatively affect you. If your pendulum says it's the wifi router causing you most trouble, keep as much distance from it as possible, wire up your devices, such as laptops, to it, rather than using them on wifi setting, and turn it all off at night for a much better sleep.

Some of the places you go throughout your day, such as your office or the shops, will have worse EMF energy than others. Again you can dowse to find out if there is negative energy in these places and either avoid them altogether, or prepare yourself when you have to go there. You can build yourself up mentally and emotionally by meditating beforehand, or physically by wearing crystals, such as black tourmaline or shungite, which absorb these energies. It's also worth spending some time 'grounding' yourself outside, with your bare feet on the earth, after every visit to these negative energy spaces and whenever you feel the need.

GEOPATHIC STRESS

Energy coming up from the earth can also affect our health and well-being, as well as that of our plants and pets. Geopathic stress is caused when the electromagnetic frequency of the earth gets distorted by natural occurrences such as underground water or mineral concentrations, fault lines or caves, or man-made electrical cables, steel pipes or underground tunnels, such as for water or sewerage. These all affect the earth's energy and can cause illness in anyone living or working above it.

If you or your pets are always unwell, can't sleep properly or are constantly irritable, and you can't get to the bottom of it, it could be down to geopathic stress. Use your pendulum to find out if your home or workspace suffers from this 'sick building syndrome' and

try to avoid the area directly above it by rearranging your furniture. Follow the tips on page 115 to cut down other electro-magnetic pollution and always unplug electrical items when not in use.

LEY LINES

Ley lines are a grid of earth energy lines criss-crossing all over the planet, often linking key sites of antiquity such as Stonehenge, the Avebury stone circles and Glastonbury Tor, as well as the prehistoric cemetery at Newgrange in Ireland, and other standing stone sites around the world. These ancient sacred sites were often positioned where ley lines meet, creating a powerful vortex of energy above, amplifying spiritual and physical energy and intention. Time spent here will connect you to the power of the natural world and our ancient past, usually leaving you feeling empowered and uplifted.

These original places of worship of Mother Earth and Father Sky are great places to go with your pendulum, especially a crystal one, to see if you can pick up on the powerful energy there. At the centre of famous sites such as Stonehenge and Avebury, many ley lines intersect, amplifying the energy at that spot.

Simply stroll around the site asking your pendulum to show you the epicentre of the energy lines. It might

spin fast one way and then the other, or spiral around with the powerful vibrations present there. It is likely to display a completely different movement to when you dowse for decisions. The energy will charge up your pendulum with power. How does your body feel? It may feel like it's pulsing with vitality, and your spirit lifted with positivity.

If you struggle to sense the centre of energy but can see straight lines of standing stones leading up to the middle of the site, follow these paths as they are likely to be where the ley lines lead. Walk between these corridors of stones holding your pendulum and see where it takes you – most likely to the true centre where the ley lines cross.

Celtic festivals, such as the summer or winter solstices, Beltane – 1 May – and Samhain (Halloween), are times during the year when earth energies can be felt more strongly. So, head to a sacred site to feel the intense energy of the place during these sacred moments with the help of your pendulum. Get there at dawn and place your pendulum on a stone as the sun rises for it to be filled with the healing energy of the sun before spending the day there dowsing with it.

Don't worry if you live nowhere near an ancient site, ley lines can also be found in open land throughout the countryside, perhaps marked by a large stone on a hilltop, a natural pond or circle of ancient trees. Using your pendulum on walks outside, you can find these energy lines all over the place. Start at a rocky outcrop in a hilly area and ask your pendulum to lead you to the local ley lines.

GHOSTHUNTING

Your pendulum is a sensitive tool that you can use to pick up spirit energies. Along ley lines, there are often legends of strange sightings such as wandering monks, black dogs or horsemen, for example. So if you know of an ancient area such as the ruins of a castle or an old well overgrown with weeds, take your pendulum there to see what stories you can pick up.

Walk slowly around the area letting your pendulum swing as it likes. It may make completely different movements than normal, often exaggerated if picking up anything unusual. Close your eyes as you do this and see if any images flash into your mind, or maybe you can feel strong emotions that have built up in the place over time.

Ghosts can become attached to places if there has been strong emotion connected to their passing, and equally intense feelings thereafter, such as fear or deep sorrow. So you may be able to tune into them using the method just described. If not, try using psychometry – picking up psychic energy from objects connected to a place or person.

USING PSYCHOMETRY AND DOWSING

Usually psychometry would involve touching an object to tune in to its energy or the energy of the person who owned it or used it often, but with ancient artefacts this can sometimes be difficult in places like museums. In a castle or a stately home, however, you can hopefully use your pendulum to dowse over the top of historical objects, in situ, and see what sights, sounds, smells, or even tastes, you can sense. If an artefact has been there a long time, ghostly presences may be attached to it that you can try to tune into as you dowse.

A crystal pendulum is best for this purpose. You want to hold it, on a short chain, about 5cm above the object and let it move freely. It may move back and forth as usual and then vibrate, or change movement quite clearly, when it connects with another dimension. It doesn't really matter what movement it makes, it's just an indicator to you to start tuning in to whatever the object wants to reveal to you.

Local industry or 'history through the ages' museums are often full of various, interesting, old objects and you can walk around, holding your pendulum to see what you can tune in to. In some such museums,

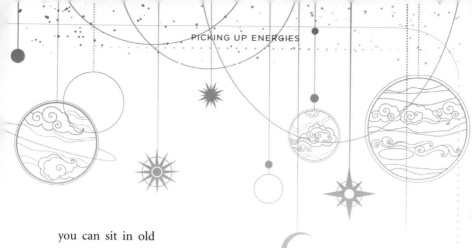

you can sit in old
buses or at school desks,
for example, where you can use your
pendulum to pick up any psychic energies there.

In these types of places, you might sometimes feel cold spots when standing still and dowsing, which can mean a presence from the spirit world is near. It's not anything to be scared of, just two dimensions meeting. If you do suddenly sense a drop in temperature for no obvious reason, hold your pendulum over the closest artefact to you and you may see or sense the presence, or hear their story unfolding in your mind. Don't think about it too much, just let the sensations or images unfold.

A WORD OF WARNING

After any kind of dowsing for spirits, say thank you to anyone who revealed themselves and wish them well, but state very clearly that you now want to stop contact and that the interaction has ended. As ghosts usually attach themselves to places, they are almost certain to stay where you found them, but it's essential to mark the end of such inter-dimensional connection to avoid being open to any negative energies or spirit attachment.

* You may want to pause for a moment and clear your energy completely, by taking some deep breaths and imagining a white light filling your aura around your body.

* Take time to ground yourself back into the present moment by feeling your feet planted firmly on the floor and having a drink or something to eat afterwards.

* When you get home, be sure to cleanse your pendulum thoroughly using the techniques on pages 36–37.

* If you are uneasy about carrying out this type of dowsing without prior experience, research it well first. You could even join in a local group of ghost-hunters or spirit dowsers to work with other like-minded people who will know the correct way of dowsing for spirits in order to stay safe.

Spiritual development

Already, after all this work with your pendulum, you are exploring your spiritual side. Tapping into your intuition, seeing images in your mind when dowsing and sensing what your pendulum is telling you, are all great ways to expand your deeper self.

Now, if you wish and are ready, you can dowse to develop this aspect of your life even further. It's all about discovering a deeper happiness and fulfilment in life, finding a purpose that motivates you more, maybe helping others in the process, and certainly boosting your own well-being in ways you never even thought possible.

However, it is not an area to be taken lightly. Finding out and acting on your spiritual path can take you in a completely different direction to the one your life is currently going in. Many people leave high-flying careers or very well-paid jobs to volunteer in developing countries, ashrams or charity projects. Perhaps you've already had longings to try something different to enrich your soul, but you keep putting it off due to lack of time, money or anxiety over leaving loved ones in the lurch if you follow your spiritual dreams.

Realising that there is more to life that the daily grind of *work, eat, sleep, repeat,* with a bit of shopping thrown in, is both empowering and destabilising. If it's all you've ever known, you may feel disorientated and confused about doing things differently. You must be prepared for change, which is naturally unsettling but can be exciting, too, especially when leading towards something better. With the help of your pendulum giving you guidance along the way, you can trust that you will be moving into a richer, more inspiring, interesting and nourishing way of living.

PREPARE PROPERLY

Preparation for learning about your spiritual path is crucial. Spend time every day meditating and getting in touch with your deepest feelings. It is here that you will get ideas to learn more about something that you may always have been interested in but never pursued, or feel a strong yearning to act on an inspiration that suddenly and persistently keeps coming to mind. Pay attention to your desires for your spiritual development and use these to form questions to ask your pendulum for help.

Maybe you want to learn more yoga, even train to become a teacher, but should you go to India to do this, or is there a better course closer to home? Perhaps you love to dance, and have always wanted to try a spiritual dance practice such as 5 rhythms or biodanza but are not sure which one would be best for you, where to do it, who with and so on. Use your pendulum to ask clear and concise questions to lead you to the best option for you right now.

When dowsing about your spiritual development, always make sure you're asking questions when you're in a calm and centred state. If you have been wanting a career change for a while, and you've just had another argument at work, it may seem like the perfect time to ask your pendulum for help with your spiritual path. But, as with all dowsing but especially this potentially life-changing area, a relaxed and neutral disposition is required.

1 Take some time to really focus your mind on your spiritual development, by doing some yoga, sitting in meditation or even

just having a long soak in the bath by candlelight to soothe your soul and bring tranquility back before you begin this important self-exploration.

2 Now, sit in your quiet space and focus on your breathing, taking deep breaths in, and letting them out slowly and gently.

3 Let your mind clear itself of any thoughts and try to remain detached from any emotions you may have about the outcome of this dowsing session.

4 Hold your pendulum chain firmly between your index finger and thumb, allowing your wrist to relax.

5 You may want to check in with your pendulum and ask it to confirm its positive and negative responses once more, especially since this is an important line of enquiry that you are undertaking.

6 Ask your pendulum if this is a good time to ask questions about your spiritual path. If 'yes', then begin to ask your questions.

7 The answer may lead to something that seems simple, such as doing more research into Buddhism, or to volunteer with a charity that you care about. But will this mean travelling the world or will you be able to do this nearer to your home? Ask for details, as required.

Whatever the outcome, be gentle with yourself through the deep changes you make, and know that your higher power – whatever you understand that to be – is supporting you. Ultimately, you are on a path to true fulfilment and happiness, so enjoy the journey above all – and let your pendulum help you along the way.

THE CHARTS

Using charts

Y ou can dowse over many other different charts, plotting your possible options around a circular or semi-circlular diagram.

If you want very detailed answers and have the time, you can use the semi-circular chart with letters of the alphabet drawn on it (see page 152), asking your pendulum to spell out answers in much the same way as a Ouija board would be used.

Alternatively, in addition to the eight charts given in the next section, you can create any number of your own charts with the possible answers

– approximately between 15 and 25 – written in segments around the circle in a counter-clockwise direction.

This is particularly good when you have many possible options you want to choose from, such as a list of many different types of yoga classes or a variety of useful herbs to supplement your diet with or to help heal an ailment. In a similar way to writing the options onto separate pieces of paper and dowsing over each one, you could write them onto a circular chart. Or if you have fewer possible answers to a question, plot them along a semi-circle to dowse over.

With all of these ways of using charts to discover your answers, the method of dowsing is still the same:

* Ask if now is the right time to dowse.

* Take some time to relax your mind and body, breathing deeply and connecting to your core.

* Ask your questions in a simple and direct fashion.

* Either dowse over each answer and watch your pendulum for its response or hold the pendulum at the centre of the circle and see where it moves to most definitively.

* Note down the 'yes' or 'no' responses if you wish.

Chart 1

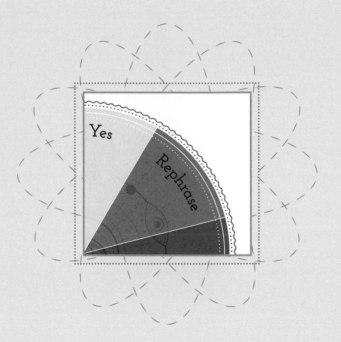

Open-ended questions with lots of negatives within them will not give you a clear answer.

How you ask a question is vitally important to successful pendulum dowsing. Open-ended questions with lots of negatives within them will not give you a clear answer. It is best to ask questions that have a direct 'yes' or 'no' answer. You should already have connected with your pendulum and discovered which direction is 'yes' and which is 'no' in its answers (see pages 44–48), but if you're not quite getting a definitive answer, you can try the chart on page 150 to see if you should rephrase your question.

You can also use this chart to confirm what you have already understood the answer to be from the usual swing for 'yes' or 'no'. It might be that your usual way to receive a 'yes' answer is directly opposite to the way it should swing for it to be a 'yes' on the chart. The pendulum will swing correctly for the right answer, even if it means it is swinging in opposite directions between a question asked normally and one with a chart underneath it.

Chart 2 – Compass

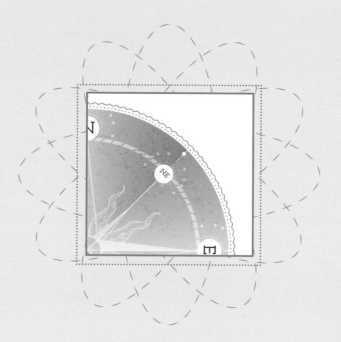

Sometimes you want to ask a question that relates to either discovering which direction you should go in or with regard to finding something that is lost. The Compass chart on page 151 will enable you to discover which direction to go in, both literally and metaphorically. For example, you could ask which direction in relation to where you are currently standing/facing is a particular thing you've lost. This can be tricky for animals and people as they can be on the move, but if you've lost a piece of jewellery, for example, this method will enable you to see which part of the room or house you should concentrate your search in.

On a less literal level, you can attribute certain options to different directions...

On a less literal level, you can attribute certain options to different directions such as 'go to university' in the East and 'get a job' in the South 'work from home' for the West and 'start a business' for the North. How you attribute each option can be arbitary or it can relate to some aspect of the direction, for example if the university you have in mind is in the East of the city or the country you live in.

Chart 3 – Alphabet

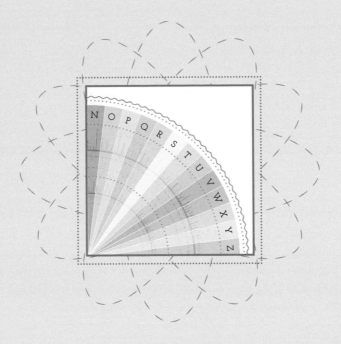

The Alphabet chart (page 152) takes a bit of patience to work with as you have 26 different options and they are very close to one another. You can blow up the chart onto larger paper if you find it easier to work with larger segments. You will find, though, that once you get the hang of it, you will know which letter is being indicated.

...you are connecting with knowledge from a Universal wisdom rather than from spirits...

You can initially ask just for a single letter that gives you the start of the name of, for example, a person or company you might want to work with or a person you might want to date. Then, if you want a more definitive answer, ask for the whole word to be spelled out.

Some may feel anxious about using an Alphabet chart as it is quite similar in look to a Ouija board, but here you are connecting with knowledge from a Universal source of wisdom rather than from spirits so it should not put you off, and, remember, if you are concerned, imagine yourself surrounded by a big ball of white light connecting you only to positive energy.

Chart 4 – Astrological

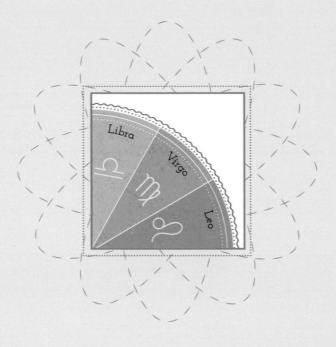

Wouldn't it be terrific to know the qualities of a future boss straight after you've been told you got the job? Or to know what sort of person you would be best suited to romantically? The Astrological chart on page 153 can provide you with those answers.

You can look up what each astrological sign is like online or in books, but remember that it is not necessarily the case that the person you are thinking of is born in that sign. It may be that they are a Gemini but have many qualities of a Leo and so the pendulum will point to Leo.

Here are some of the key qualities for each sign:

Aries – Bold and opinionated.

Taurus – Sensual, stubborn and loves security.

Gemini – Chatty, quick-witted and personable.

Cancer – Nurturing and emotional.

Leo – Glamorous and brave.

Virgo – Organised and practical.

Libra – Indecisive and charming.

Scorpio – Passionate and secretive.

Sagittarius – Loyal and freedom-loving.

Capricorn – Ambitious and laser focused.

Aquarius – Just and intelligent.

Pisces – Unpredictable and dreamy.

Discover the qualities of a future boss or someone you want to date.

Chart 5 – Days of the Week

The Days of the Week chart is on page 154. Not only can you find out exactly what day a particular event will happen (for example, when the cheque will arrive or when that person you fancy will ask you out), you can also be guided by the quality of each day since the days of the week correspond to different deities and their characters. These are:

Find out which day that cheque in the post will eventually arrive in your letterbox.

Monday – Luna, emotional connection and feminine energy.

Tuesday – Mars, facing challenges with energy and panache.

Wednesday – Mercury, great for communications and writing.

Thursday – Jupiter, expansion, prosperity and growth in all things.

Friday – Venus, romantic outcomes, beauty and joy.

Saturday – Saturn, obstacles and application of sense over sensibility.

Sunday – Apollo, music, strength and wisdom. Also, traditionally the day of rest in Christian societies so it may be a message to leave the question alone and just wait.

Chart 6 – Months

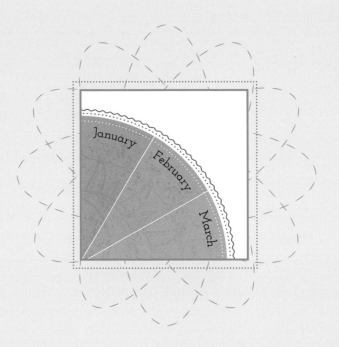

The Months chart (page 155) is very useful for finding out when bigger life events are likely to happen. It may be that you need to figure out the date for your wedding or whether your baby will be born early or late. Forewarned is forearmed so you can use this chart to give you a heads-up.

When formulating your question, you can also ask for advice as to which month is best for your particular query. For example, you could ask which month would be best for you to go on holiday to a particular destination. The pendulum will give you an indication of when the weather is likely to be best and will also indicate any unforseen problems such as cancellations or closures.

If you want to see which month you should put your house on sale, you can focus the energy further by putting your house key on the centre of the chart and dowsing with your pendulum above it. If you wonder whether your answer is the month indicated by the front swing of your pendulum or the back, in the case of it going back and forth, you will find a sensation of 'pull' coming from one segment over another. Over time, you will become more adept at knowing exactly what your pendulum is trying to tell you since your connection to it increases the more you work with it.

> You will become more adept at knowing what your pendulum is telling you over time.

Chart 7 – Numbers

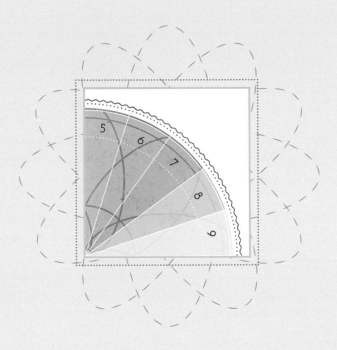

The Numbers chart (page 156) will enable you to discover everything from your ideal lottery numbers to how many dates you will have with a prospective beau. When you require a double digit number, ask that you be given two numbers and dowse separately for the two. If, as in the example above of the lottery, you get a figure that is higher than what you can enter – say 76 for a ticket that only goes up to 59, you can add the two numbers together to get your answer. So 7+6 = 13.

Discover your ideal lottery numbers or even the age at which you might retire.

You can also ask what age you will be when certain things you want to have happen will occur so the question 'what age will I retire?' might get you a double figure that is earlier than you thought. If you get a deeply unrealistic answer, you might want to keep practising as a good sign that you have not properly connected to your pendulum can be getting humorously unlikely answers.

Chart 8 – Percentages

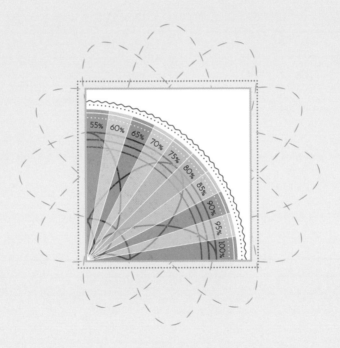

Find out the percentage you are likely to get of any ideal figure you have in your mind.

The Percentages chart (page 157) is perfect for checking the likelihood of something happening that you are not getting a clear 'yes' or 'no' answer for. It can also give you more detail for a question where you know an ideal figure (for example, what you would like your salary to be after a promotion negotiation) and you want to know what percentage of it you are likely to achieve after discussions.

A good barometer to see how this chart works is to try it with the likelihood of rain and see what percentage it gives you. Then check your local weather forecast to see if the two match up. You will be surprised at how accurately the two marry up, once you are using your pendulum with confidence.

You can also check if you have the right level of a micronutrient or vitamin as it will swing to 100 per cent if you have the right amount in your body. Of course, you should always consult a medical professional if you have any queries about your health.

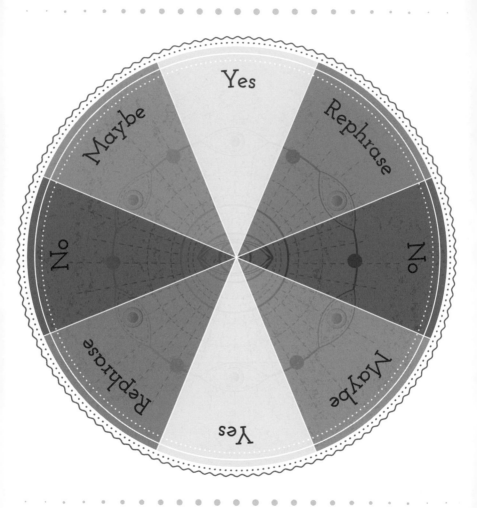

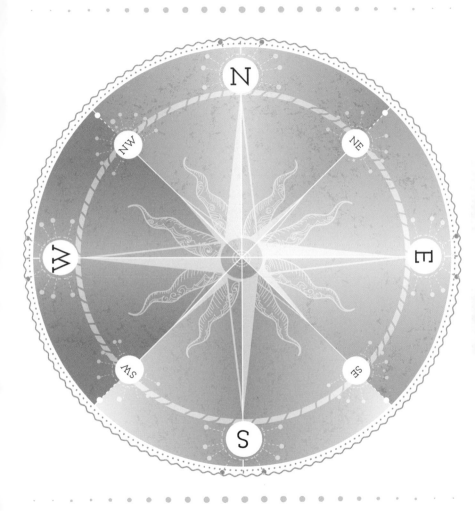

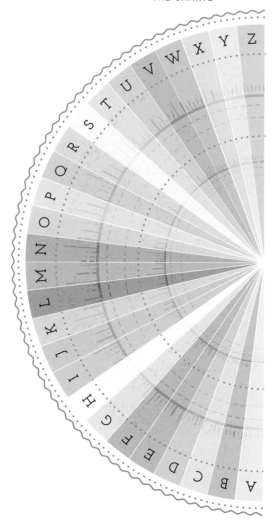

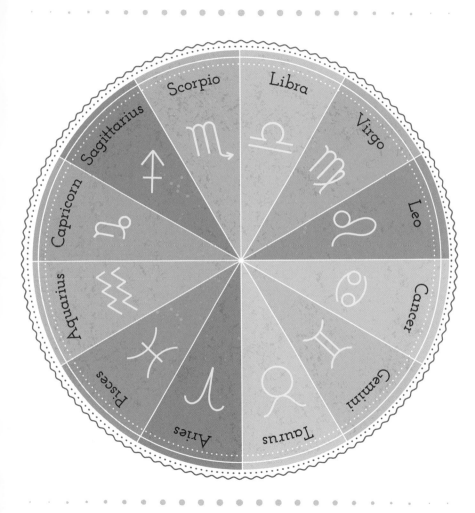

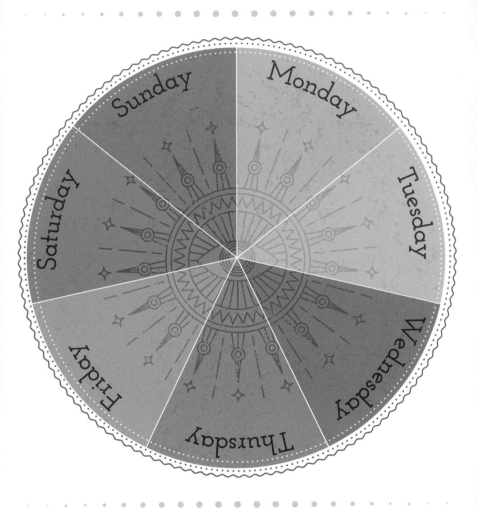

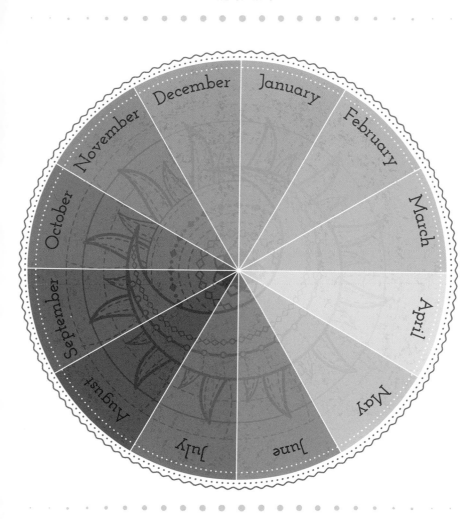

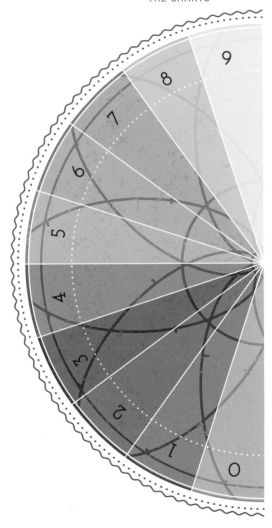

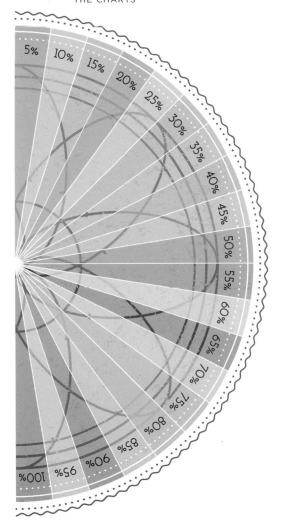

Further reading

Books

Eason, Cassandra *Pendulum Dowsing* (Piatkus, 2008)
Hunt, Brenda *A Beginner's Guide to Pendulum Dowsing* (Self-published, 2012)
Hunter, Erich *Pendulum Healing* (Self-published, 2015)
Sonnenberg, Petra *The Great Pendulum Book* (Sterling, 2015)

Online resources

pendulumalchemy.com
readprint.com/chapter-35044/Custom-and-Myth-Andrew-Lang

Organisations

The British Society of Dowsers: britishdowsers.org